INDECENT LIBERTIES

INDECENT LIBERTIES

Robert Schmuhl

University of Notre Dame Press
Notre Dame, Indiana

Library of Congress Cataloging-in-Publication Data

Schmuhl, Robert.
    Indecent liberties / Robert Schmuhl.
       p.   cm.
    Independent bibliographical references and index.
    ISBN 0–268–01216–4 (cl. : alk. paper)
    1. United States—Moral conditions. 2. Hyperbole—Social
aspects—United States. 3. Liberty—Social aspects—United States.
I. Title.
HN90.M6S349 1999
306′.0973—dc21   99–35183

To
Thomas J. Stritch
and
Max Lerner (1902–1992)
more than teachers
more than friends

CONTENTS

INTRODUCTION

The central idea of this book—that Americans have a continuing penchant for going to extremes in ways that produce debatable, if not deplorable, consequences—first occurred to me in 1972. At the time I happened to be in graduate school (studying American literature and history). In addition, and probably more influential to my rumination then, I also worked as a journalist for newspapers and magazines. Whether I spent more time as a reporter than as a student is between me and God.

Covering the turbulence of the late 1960s and early 1970s, I had witnessed racial violence in the streets—at one point almost being shot by a former high-school classmate who had become a police officer—and seen the upheaval on several college campuses. America was off kilter, anyone could observe, but the why of it all and the possible relationship to the past became a nagging concern.

Subsequently, while trying to combine academic and journalistic writing assignments, I kept confronting examples of this (for lack of another term) character trait in contemporary popular culture, political life, social thinking, and group activity. Several essays appearing in this book attempt to make sense of the recent past at the same time that they pursue the larger, unifying theme of going too far, of pushing thought or action beyond prudent limits.

To call the principal argument of this volume "the wretched excess thesis" (as one friend dubbed it) elevates what I'm doing to a theoretical status I find uncomfortably rarefied. As we see throughout academic life today, intellectual rigidity tends to sterilize theory, removing much of its value and meaning. It is true, however, that the notion of "wretched excess"—or what I refer to as the taking of indecent liberties—recurs so frequently in American life that it deserves sorting out and speculation on a sustained scale.

To be sure, you find intimations of this theme in other works. Thorstein Veblen's first book, *The Theory of the Leisure Class* (1899), described—and satirized—the consequences of Gilded Age capitalism by focusing on "conspicuous leisure" and "conspicuous consumption." To those who gain much, Veblen argues, there is what he rightly calls "conspicuous waste," the showy spending for status. In 1954, at a time when Americanist scholars were probing distinctive traits of this country and its citizens, David M. Potter published *People of Plenty: Economic Abundance and the American Character.* With acute perception and working in the "zone where history and the behavioral sciences meet," Potter explored how wealth of various kinds—or in his recurring word "abundance"—"influenced American life in many ways." For example, our notions of equality and democracy, in his view, are (to a considerable degree) shaped by the reality or potentiality of abundance.

It is possible to build on Potter's analysis and argument to look more broadly at the subject of excess, the carrying of the existing abundance in whatever realm to extremes. Joseph Heller's memorable portrayal of Milo Minderbinder in the novel *Catch-22* is a savagely funny statement of the American Dream gone wild. Consummate plotter for profits and positions even in wartime, Minderbinder lampoons the make-a-buck-at-any-cost mentality that Heller finds dangerous. To corner the Egyptian cotton market to provide chocolate-covered cotton for the troops to eat is a ridiculous way of selling cotton candy. However, such antics earn for Milo the admiration of Americans and foreigners alike. Heller's dark comedy draws into question the lengths to which a wheeler-and-dealer in a free enterprise system will go for the sake of more money and power. When soldiers die as a result of Minderbinder's schemes, we all see the ironic hollowness of

Milo's slogan: "What's good for M & M Enterprises is good for the country."

Heller's criticism notwithstanding, some commentators on the United States will say the dynamism animating this country makes the possibility for overstepping previously set boundaries a natural consequence of a robustly free society. They are right, but it is necessary to add that contemporary forces (such as the rapidly expanding information technologies) accelerate circumstances to an extent that they often spin out of control, undercutting the original merit of an idea, cause, or action. Recognizing potential dangers is an initial step in attempting to avoid them.

From the outrageous hoaxes and nonstop hoopla of P. T. Barnum's American Museum and, later, his "greatest show on earth" in the nineteenth century to today's most sophisticatedly produced Hollywood blockbuster extravaganza, excess is endemic in our popular culture. To celebrate the one hundredth birthday of the Statue of Liberty in 1986, seventy-five Elvis Presley look-alikes performed simultaneously on a New York stage. Given the circumstances and the symbolic power of the Statue, one such imitator might have been one too many.

Moreover, the hyping of events or spectacles to gain public attention now goes to such extraordinary lengths that our reaction is often ho-hum. Las Vegas has become an entire metropolis dedicated to excess to entice people into a desert to part with their money in every imaginable way (and a few unimaginable ones). Regardless of the sport, each athletic season seems to bring at least one "game of the decade." Every other year, "a battle of the century" takes place. Although such manifestations of immoderation have a certain significance, I am more interested in examining larger forces or movements and their impact on the America we know—and the America of the twenty-first century. I worry that sensory overload will become desensitizing, with excess of whatever kind boringly commonplace.

In a *Paris Review* interview that was published fall 1969, E. B. White described the imbalance he perceived in contemporary literature, hinting at the consequences of this work:

> A writer must reflect and interpret his society, his world;
> he must also provide inspiration and guidance and challenge.
> Much writing today strikes me as deprecating, destructive, and
> angry. There are good reasons for anger, and I have nothing
> against anger. But I think some writers have lost their sense of
> proportion, their sense of humor, and their sense of apprecia-
> tion. I am often mad, but I would hate to be nothing but mad:
> and I think I would lose what little value I may have as a writer
> if I were to refuse, as a matter of principle, to accept the warm-
> ing rays of the sun, and to report them, whenever, and if ever,
> they happen to strike me. (p. 86)

American writers, of course, are not alone in lacking a "sense of
proportion." Mae West's wisecrack—"Too much of a good thing
can be wonderful"—describes this country's conspicuous con-
spicuousness with a wry sagacity.

Interestingly, going to excess is not exclusively a one-way
street to greater acquisitiveness, the outer limits of previously established boundaries, or a level of hype beyond a flamboyant producer's over-heated imagination. Although much less frequently,
in America you also have the other extreme, embodied, most notably, in the life and philosophy of Henry David Thoreau. In
Walden, he famously urged: "Simplicity, simplicity, simplicity! I
say, let your affairs be as two or three, and not a hundred or a
thousand; instead of a million count half a dozen, and keep your
accounts on your thumbnail. . . . Simplify, simplify." Thoreau
goes on to advocate a more refined sense of proportion, a call
that is repeated in this volume with much less eloquence—and
much less dramatic personal experience.

There are those who will say artists like Thoreau form the
avant-garde in any culture and that they cultivate the extremes
to produce new and distinctive work. This, of course, is true;
however, the matter becomes more complicated when one lives
as today in what has been frequently called "a culture of excess."
In an August 2, 1998 essay, *New York Times* art critic Michael
Kimmelman observed, "It's rare to feel really shocked by anything in art now, shock having been the aim of so much of what's

on view for so long that it has become a cliché, which poses the obvious problem that clichés by their nature aren't shocking." As art without limits can become chaos, so too in other areas a sense of individual and collective moral responsibility becomes vital. Otherwise there is the danger of always operating at or being exposed to the most extreme position in a constantly changing environment. What are the limits in an era without limits?

Much of the work on this volume took place—fittingly enough—amid the unfolding story of President Bill Clinton's involvement with former White House intern Monica Lewinsky and other charges of misconduct. When people inquired about work-in-progress and I mentioned the phrase "indecent liberties," they invariably associated the president's travail with the title. The comportment of the president, Congress, the Office of Independent Counsel Kenneth Starr, and the media led to such a conclusion. Geneva Overholser, a syndicated columnist for the *Washington Post,* pointed out on October 10, 1998, that many members of the House of Representatives who voted to keep sexually explicit material off the Internet favored release of every word of intimate information about the president's extramarital behavior: "When it comes to sex, lurching between extremes is what we do in America. We are a society torn between prurience and prudishness, libertinism and stern disapproval. Not that this lurching lands us somewhere in the middle. We just keep lurching."

The first and last essays of this book are new and attempt to provide a conceptual framework and conclusion for the other pieces that have appeared previously in somewhat different forms. In preparing the earlier efforts for inclusion here, I have not only recast certain sentences to clarify an idea or argument, to include relevant references, or to remove redundancies but also provided postscript statements concerning the essay's original composition and, in most instances, additional reflections to update the subject from the perspective of the late 1990s. A few points, I confess, are repeated, but this is done deliberately for the sake of emphasis, continuity, and unity.

To a certain extent, some of the essays seem to be prose snap-shots of a distinct time or contemporary circumstance. That, alas, is in the nature of writing about the here and now. But, for better or for worse, the larger point or argument of this book hovers over each page, providing either a haunting or a hypo-thetical unity. You, dear reader, can take your pick.

LIFE, LIBERTY, AND THE PURSUIT OF EXCESS

To wander across America is to see (if not quite believe) what Gertrude Stein meant when she wrote:

> In the United States there is more space where nobody is than where anybody is.
> This is what makes America what it is.

This sense of space, of vast and varied territory, extends backward in time to the first encounters between Native Americans and European settlers. From the perspective of those who risked everything for a different existence elsewhere, their New World offered not only a fresh start but endless elbow-room. To be sure, wilderness abounded. A squirrel, someone later remarked, could jump tree-to-tree from the Atlantic Ocean to the Mississippi River without touching the ground. But the freedom coming from "more space" worked with other freedoms the settlers were nurturing, and it had lasting consequence.

The ability to pick up and move elsewhere to begin life anew became an American prerogative. Geographical abundance whetted other appetites, which the closing of the frontier near the end of the nineteenth century did not suppress and which were vividly described (among other places) in "tall tales," with their emphasis on superhuman traits and reality-defying grandeur. The wide-openness of the land that over time became the United States helped create a love of bigness in other aspects of life. As a young Theodore Roosevelt asserted in a Fourth of July speech in 1886 out in the Dakota Territory, " . . . like all Americans, I like big things; big prairies, big forests and mountains, big wheat-fields, railroads—and herds of cattle, too—big factories, steamboats, and everything else."

Roosevelt, however, went on to temper his pride with a warning that, in its way, continues to have resonance and meaning:

> But we must keep steadily in mind that no people were ever yet benefited by riches if their prosperity corrupted their virtue. It is of more importance that we should show ourselves honest, brave, truthful, and intelligent than that we should own all the railways and grain elevators in the world. We have fallen heirs to the most glorious heritage a people ever received and each one must do his part if we wish to show that the nation is worthy of its good fortune. (in Hagedorn, p. 410)

Using other words, TR is warning about going too far, of Americans sometimes wanting so much that acquisitiveness crowds out "virtue" (and all that might imply) along with other balancing characteristics.

What worried the irrepressible TR over a century ago has become even more troubling during the twentieth century. Indeed, to look at the whole sweep of American experience is to see a parade of excess in so many areas that trembling for the Republic in a collective St. Vitus's dance might well be the appropriate response. As Charles Paul Freund remarked in *The New Republic* (March 27, 1989), as the 1980s—described as "The Decade of Excess" in several journalistic assessments—concluded: "Nothing in moderation has been our unofficial motto for a long time, with libertine and puritan subcultures leapfrogging each other to set the tone for an unstable mainstream. If nobody expects to stamp out all vices, major or minor, it seems nonetheless to be our cyclical puritan conceit to try. The desirability of tolerating small vices so as to avoid worse ones never seems to come up, one reason why other cultures—those that have shrugged off their own utopian conceits, and those who never had any—scratch their heads at us."

In *America and Americans*, John Steinbeck is more blunt and personal in assessing his fellow citizens: "For the most part we are an intemperate people: we eat too much when we can, drink too much, indulge our senses too much. Even in our so-called virtues we are intemperate: a teetotaler is not content not to drink—he must stop all the drinking in the world; a vegetarian among us would outlaw the eating of meat. We work too hard, and many die under the strain; and then to make up for that we play with a violence as suicidal." Steinbeck's scattershot criticism lacks nuance; however, he acknowledges the constant interplay between vices and virtues, a communion that becomes important in discussing the broader implications of American excess.

Interestingly, in case after case the origin of what ultimately gets taken to an extreme, even absurd, degree makes sense or seems well-meaning. Who, for example, could have predicted that the temperance movement would eventually lead to the Eighteenth Amendment to the Constitution and to fourteen years of Prohibition? That organized crime became an ominous and continuing force in American life as a result of the government ban on alcohol is a case study of unintended consequences darkly overshadowing the good intentions of trying to correct a social problem by using political means. It would be impossible to argue that the extremism of the reform accomplished more good than the countervailing evil of illegality that took root and still flourishes. Actually, in retrospect, running contraband booze to fuel the Roaring Twenties seems a lesser sin than the other vices (gambling, prostitution, drugs) crime families became involved in as they amassed power during Prohibition.

As the historian Richard Hofstadter observes with characteristic insight (in the preface to Andrew Sinclair's *Era of Excess: A Social History of the Prohibition Movement*) about the "ironies" of this period:

> Before prohibition became law, the prohibitionists decried alcohol as a form of deadly poison. After prohibition was law, they approved the legal poisoning of industrial alcohol, knowing full well that men would die from drinking it. Excess had this way of turning things into their opposites: an amenity became a crime; the imposition of controls led to a loss of control; the

churches created gangsters; reformers became reactionaries; purifiers became poisoners. Excess also made it impossible for the politicians to fulfill their customary function of compromising opposed interests and mediating between extremes. That some men may live by principle is possible only because others live by compromise. Excess destroyed this nice symbiosis: it converted the politician into a bogus man of principle, a breed of hypocrite who voted one way while he drank the other. (pp. vii–viii)

If hypocrisy is the politician's cardinal sin, Prohibition was a time like no other. In the White House and elsewhere, the law was a joke, with less meaning than what resulted in response to it. Extremists won, but at what price?

It is difficult to imagine the nation's founders debating—or even contemplating—legislation to outlaw alcohol. They not only had better things to do, they emphasized in their public work such classical virtues as restraint, simplicity, and balance. The Constitution, with its three branches of government set up to check abusive excesses of power, endures as a plea for equilibrium and for dividing the responsibilities of public business. In a 1798 letter, Jefferson cheered the prospect of state governments functioning in similar fashion to the federal system, operating "like the planets revolving round their common sun, acting and acted upon according to their respective weights and distances" to "produce that beautiful equilibrium on which our Constitution is founded. . . . " Praising "a degree of perfection, unexampled but in the planetary system itself," he went on to remark: "The enlightened statesman, therefore, will endeavor to preserve the weight and influence of every part, as too much given to any member of it would destroy the general equilibrium." To attempt to go too far is to risk judicial or political correction. Franklin D. Roosevelt learned this from the Congress with its rejection of his scheme in 1937 to "pack" the Supreme Court with justices friendly to his initiatives. Bill Clinton's Democratic Party lost control of both houses of the Congress in the mid-term election of 1994 in large measure as a reaction to his proposed health-care plan that many voters perceived as overly intrusive and expensive.

At almost the same time as the Constitution was becoming the law of the new republic, Benjamin Franklin in his *Autobiography* and other writings was championing personal traits he thought readers should follow in leading successful lives. In *The Autobiography,* he set down thirteen specific "virtues" and added "precepts" for amplification. Here are a few of his "virtues":

¶1. Temperance. Eat not to dullness; drink not to elevation.
¶3. Order. Let all your things have their places; let each part of your business have its time.
¶5. Frugality. Make no expense but to do good to others or yourself; *i.e.,* waste nothing.
¶9. Moderation. Avoid extremes; forbear resenting injuries so much as you think they deserve.
¶12. Chastity. Rarely use venery but for health or offspring, never to dullness, weakness, or the injury of your own or another's peace or reputation. (pp. 93–95)

Given what is now known of Franklin's private life, including the existence of at least two illegitimate children, the remarks about chastity seem posthumously ironic. However, the "virtues" conform to the times and represent common, acceptable thinking for citizens establishing a nation unlike any other that previously existed. Individual freedom and liberty formed the cornerstone for political, economic, and religious actions, but personal virtues were expected to temper the extent to which the people enjoyed their freedom and liberty.

Despite the institutional impediments to governmental excess and the moral guidance of such celebrated figures as Franklin to maintain self-control, America's earliest days were not without public and memorable examples of going too far. This phenomenon recurs with extravagant ostentation in the newspapers of that time. To be sure, many existed as megaphones for political interests, and participants in the partisan press knew that the sharper their criticism of the opposition, the greater the potential impact on the reading public.

Franklin's own grandson, Benjamin Franklin Bache, represents the approach often taken in what were then called "the public prints." Writing for the *Philadelphia Aurora,* Bache left little doubt about his thinking—and what he said strikes someone today as at a certain variance from the restraint or control of his grandfather's virtues. For example, you might expect a valediction—however modest or even grudging—when George Washington left the presidency. No, in the March 6, 1797 *Aurora,* Bache sent the father of the country to his retirement at Mount Vernon by saying: " . . . the man who is the source of all the misfortunes of our country, is this day reduced to a level with his fellow citizens, and is no longer possessed of power to multiply evils upon the United States. If ever there was a period for rejoicing, this is the moment—every heart in unison with the freedom and happiness of the people ought to beat high, with exultation that the name of Washington from this day ceases to give a currency to political iniquity, and to legalize corruption." Bache continues with a bill of particulars, building to "this day ought to be a *jubilee* in the United States."

The First Amendment, of course, permitted journalists to criticize anyone perceived as a political opponent with impunity. A free press coexisted with other fundamental freedoms. Even before the ratification of the Bill of Rights in 1791, Thomas Jefferson observed, "Were it left to me to decide whether we should have government without newspapers or newspapers without government, I should not hesitate for a moment to prefer the latter." Two decades later and near the end of his second term as president, Jefferson had been on the receiving end of so many journalistic brickbats (and the subject of so many scandalous rumors) that his mind has decidedly changed. In a letter he wrote: "Nothing can now be believed which is seen in a newspaper. Truth itself becomes suspicious by being put into that polluted vehicle. The real extent of this state of misinformation is known only to those who are in situations to confront facts within their knowledge with the lies of the day. I really look with commiseration over the great body of my fellow citizens, who, reading newspapers, live and die in the belief, that they have known something of what has been passing in the world in their time. . . . "

In the two statements of Jefferson, there is what proves to be a recurring pattern in most cases of American excess. Abstract idealism (in this case sparked by the potential good of journalism serving as a sentinel on watch over government) loses out to the realities of daily, continual action. Freedom (again, in this case, the sanctioning approval of the First Amendment) allows those who are involved in a particular effort or cause to operate from an extreme position. Like the example of Prohibition, the movement from original idea to ultimate execution becomes a process of reducing whatever salutary effects there might be, with the larger consequences far removed from those initially envisioned. As journalism developed and matured, political partisanship gave way to popular appeal of the Penny Press and other forms of mass communication. Instances, even periods, of excess occurred in journalism, notably the Yellow Press days a century ago and the tabloidization of news we have so much with us in recent years.

In its own peculiar and lamentable way, slavery stands alone as a scarring illustration of carrying an idea or plan too far. Unlike Prohibition or journalistic excess that have (in theory, at least) justifiable starting points, slavery is indefensible no matter what. To think that slave owners would use their freedom to deny it to others is not only morally incongruous but opposed to basic American principles. However, here we come back to the great expanse of land available for agriculture and other settlement described earlier. Such back-wrenching work demanded the persistent toil of thousands of people, with slavery becoming the preferred, most efficient method, especially (of course) on large Southern plantations.

Free-market capitalism occupies a central place in the history of slavery in America, and similar capitalistic objectives (existing within cycles featuring periods of boom and bust) drive other excesses both past and present. That it took the Civil War and its grotesqueries to finally resolve the question—and evil—of slavery should be proof enough of how damaging something carried to such an extreme can be.

However, as Paul Johnson notes in *A History of the American People,* "The end of the Civil War solved the problem of slavery and started the problem of the blacks, which is with America still." Today some of the loudest voices in the African-American community talk of the need for resegregation, the pulling away as much as possible from mainstream American culture and society for the sake of Afrocentric living. To reject the possibility of integration or assimilation is a contemporary expression of extremism as troubling as any white racist's call for separation based on some unfounded fantasy of superiority. The same environment of free thought and free speech incubates both views, which operate on the margins of American life.

Besides the Civil War in the nineteenth century, blood flowed freely in the West as settlers pushed from the Atlantic region to the Pacific Ocean. The phrase "the winning of the West" (which Theodore Roosevelt used for his multivolume history) and the popular 1962 movie titled *How the West Was Won* imply losers in the process, and losers there certainly were. More recent scholarly works—such as Patricia Nelson Limerick's *The Legacy of Conquest: The Unbroken Past of the American West* (1987), Richard White's *"It's Your Misfortune and None of My Own": A New History of the American West* (1991), David E. Stannard's *American Holocaust: The Conquest of the New World* (1992), and Paula Mitchell Marks's *In a Barren Land: American Indian Dispossession and Survival* (1998)—chronicle the consequences of westward expansion on native inhabitants, wildlife, and natural resources. The concept of conquest—of certain people overcoming, if not overwhelming, certain other people or forces to gain control—pervades the latest interpretation of what actually happened as the frontier territories became new states of the United States. Romantic western films, featuring battles between "cowboys and Indians," might continue to entertain, but their relationship to reality is at best tangential.

In coming to terms with American excess, the story of the near extermination of the bison or buffalo on the western plains stands out in bold and bloody relief. To think that an estimated seventy million bison roamed this country's land in 1800 and that only a few hundred remained a century later tests believability. Yet, for several reasons germane to this argument, the so-called "great buffalo hunt" went to that extreme. Free-market economic objectives to exploit an abundant resource subsequently converged with a cruel governmental strategy to control—or, if you will, conquer—Native Americans in the West, leading to unchecked slaughter of herd after herd of buffalo, death without end.

Early in the nineteenth century, as Wayne Gard tells it in *The Great Buffalo Hunt,* hunters went after buffalo for the value of their hides—about a dollar per hide. The meat from literally millions of buffalo was left to rot or to feed scavenger animals and birds. The hunters' work helped clear land that ranchers later used for sheep and cattle. Yet what was beneficial to hunters and ranchers proved devastating to the Native Americans of the plains. These American nomads relied on the buffalo for much that they needed—food, clothing, and shelter. Bones were even fashioned into tools. Besides the utilitarian nature of the animal to Native Americans, there was a spiritual dimension as well. An afterlife in a land abundant with buffalo was an abiding prospect of paradise among certain tribes. A white bison on earth assumed sacral power.

Given these peoples' reality and reverence, is it any wonder why they kept attacking those they perceived as the killers of their most precious resource? Winning the West became, in part, white people's sport with consequences reaching beyond the slaughter of a particular animal. As Doug Peacock observes in *Bison: Distant Thunder:* "The decision to exterminate the bison was semi-conscious. The conflict by white settler with Indians over land control was resolved when official policy linked the two: to exterminate the Indian you only needed to exterminate his commissary, the buffalo. The Army handed out free ammunition to anyone; any dude who could ride the railroad could now shoot buffalo from the train, leaving them to die and rot by the thousands."

By the late 1860s and early 1870s, when around fifteen million bison still roamed the prairies, legislative proposals in the U.S. Congress, states, and territories sought to end the wanton carnage. But these appeals had little to no effect, with the legal measures passed receiving no enforcement. In 1873, Columbus Delano, Secretary of the Interior under President U. S. Grant, wrote in an official report: "I would not seriously regret the total disappearance of the buffalo from our western prairies, in its effect upon the Indians. I would regard it rather as a means of hastening their sense of dependence upon the products of the soil and their own labors."

At the turn of the century, with just a few hundred bison still alive, a conservation movement in America finally came into being to protect the buffalo. Of course, by that time the animal was near extinction—and Native Americans had been forced onto reservations. The hides had brought wealth for some hunters and East Coast furriers, and ranchers now had vast expanses of tamed land for their livestock. Farmers could also raise fields of crops without fear that a herd of wandering animals would trample through acreage that had been planted.

In retrospect, however, what price was paid to settle the West? That question, in part, can be answered by reading revisionist studies of what is known as "the New Western History," analysis that tempers the triumphalism of earlier works. Clearly tragedies took place amid the triumphs of expansion, and what actually happened—mythic or not—deserves scrutiny. Curiously, some of the most balanced—truest, if you will—depictions of long-ago western life can be found in fiction, the novels and stories of Wallace Stegner and Larry McMurtry.

The westward movement across America affected not only the people and wildlife already living there but the earth and ground itself. In *Virgin Land: The American West as Symbol and Myth,* Henry Nash Smith explains how unpredictable rainfall and constant use of the cleared fields provoked second thoughts about the settlement of the plains. "After a half century of struggle," Smith writes, "the drought of the 1930s turned much of the settled portion of the plains into a dust bowl and raised the question whether the region had not been seriously overpopulated." To the south, in the Texas Hill Country acre upon acre of abundant grassland became barren ground (between 1860 and 1900) after giant herds of cattle overgrazed the land and left no protection for the top soil, which either blew away or washed off. In many cases, initial usage of an area went to such an extreme that the purpose and character of the area changed—and not necessarily for the better. In other cases, early lessons helped institute methods of conservation and more enlightened land-use management. The point, however, is the relative lack of thoughtful planning for the future, when opportunities of one kind or another present themselves. A let's-make-a-quick-buck attitude combines with a let-tomorrow-take-care-of-itself approach, which over time can have dire consequences.

While the West was physically changing in dramatic ways, a post–Civil War money frenzy gave rise to schemes for getting rich without parallel in the country's past. Mark Twain (along with coauthor Charles Dudley Warner) satirized the greed and corruption in *The Gilded Age: A Tale of Today,* published in 1873. As they wrote to close chapter 26 of the novel:

> Beautiful credit! The foundation of modern society. Who shall say that this is not the golden age of mutual trust, of unlimited reliance upon human promises? That is a peculiar condition of society which enables a whole nation to instantly recognize point and meaning in the familiar newspaper anecdote, which puts into the mouth of a distinguished speculator in lands and mines this remark:—"I wasn't worth a cent two years ago, and now I owe two millions of dollars." (p. 193)

Making fun of the mania for money that existed during the Gilded Age might have been profitable sport for Mark Twain as a writer. However, Samuel Clemens, the creator of the authorial persona the public admired as Mark Twain, became a notorious victim of the times he deftly lampooned. Eager to enjoy the material success he saw around him, Clemens started a publishing house and invested heavily in a typesetting machine—and ended up declaring bankruptcy in 1894. The dark, pessimistic humor of Mark Twain's later writings is, in part, an expression of his personal problems as a financial failure.

Other people, of course, prospered in this environment's robust lack of restraint. If the phrase "robber baron" sounds overly pejorative, figures such as John D. Rockefeller, J. Pierpont Morgan, and Andrew Carnegie built business empires that, in their way, redefined free-market capitalism in the United States. As government officials stood aside—often with their hands out—to let the private sector develop, captains of industry created corporate empires of unprecedented wealth and power.

The super rich of that era, with their enormous estates and private railroad cars, went about their lives in stark contrast to people of lesser means, especially the burgeoning number of new immigrants crowding the tenement buildings in cities and former African-American slaves subsisting in squalid surroundings in the South and elsewhere. At this time, chronicled by Ray Ginger in *Age of Excess: The United States from 1877–1914*, racial, class, and ethnic divisions sharpen more vividly than at earlier periods in the nation's history. The growing differences between the haves and have-nots provoked concern, and publication of Jacob A. Riis's *How the Other Half Lives* in 1890 focused attention on the plight of slum-dwelling New Yorkers.

A revealing event of this time was the 1893 Columbian Exposition in Chicago, which featured the presentation of historian Frederick Jackson Turner's paper about the significance of the American frontier and "White City" with its wondrous exhibits of human progress and invention. Although "White City" projected the image of purity, an uncorrupted place of unified neoclassical forms on a grand scale, the illusion of marble structures masked the reality of buildings slapped together with plaster, hemp, and horse hair and then painted a uniform white. In a way, the façade symbolized the deeper meaning of the time. As Alan Trachtenberg perceptively points out in *The Incorporation of America: Culture and Society in the Gilded Age,* "For a summer's moment, White City had seemed the fruition of a nation, a culture, a whole society: the celestial city of man set upon a hill for all the world to behold. It seemed the triumph of America itself, the old republican ideal. But dressed now in empty Roman orders, that ideal had taken on another look and signified another meaning: the alliance and incorporation of business, politics, industry, and culture." This triumph, though, comes at a price, according to Trachtenberg: "It seemed the victory of elites in business, politics, and culture over dissident but divided voices of labor, farmers, immigrants, blacks and women." The "Gilded Age" or the "Age of Excess" exacerbated an environment of extremes, setting in motion forces that in the future would accelerate and produce additional examples of excess throughout the twentieth century.

Looking back at certain periods, movements, or even events in American life, there is an indigenous pattern or trait that often exposes the underside of freedom. A stimulus of some kind—either idealistic or capitalistic in the main—sparks action that over time spins out of control, making it difficult to recognize the original reason or goal for the activity. In some instances, over-reaction or going to an extreme occurs quickly. The Japanese bombed Pearl Harbor on December 7, 1941. Two months later, President Franklin Roosevelt issued Executive Order 9066, which led to the internment of some 120,000 Japanese-Americans in ten prison-like camps in remote areas of California, Arizona, Colorado, Idaho, Wyoming, Utah, and Arkansas. Fear and war fever reached such intensity in a matter of days that citizens lost their freedom for three years in a clear example of the government going too far.

Popular communications in recent years provide a continuing case study in taking advantage of new money-making outlets within the broader context of an environment that allows free expression. As cable and satellite delivery expanded viewing options and VCR technology made watching movies and other tapes common occurrences, there was an industry-wide scramble to adapt. The major television networks—ABC, CBS, NBC, and Fox—moved away from broadcasting programs of the so-called "least objectionable" variety. The trick was to find fare that gathered viewers from the most advertiser-favorable demographic groups.

The shrinkage of the captive audience, which previously existed when ABC, CBS, and NBC dominated the medium, resulted in more explicit—yes, extreme—fare from mainstream providers. Soap operas (shown during both the day and evening) became steamier, and the phrase "trash TV" took on more generalized meaning beyond the syndicated talk shows devoted to abnormal psychology and behavior. In *The Beast, the Eunuch and the Glass-Eyed Child,* Pulitzer Prize-winning television critic Ron Powers notes:

> American commercial television has struck a bargain with the dark gods that is worthy, in some respects, of Greek tragedy. It seems doomed to reach ever outward, at peril of its audiences' satiety, toward new extremes of shock and vulgarity and self-abasement—only to find that those extremes have been absorbed within weeks into the fabric of the commonplace. And so it must reach out again. . . .
>
> Television as we know it, in other words, is fated forever to be a victim of its own excess. I cannot conceive of a corrective arising from "the marketplace," nor can I imagine a formula mandated by the government that would not do violence to the principle of free expression, however debased that principle has become in practice. (pp. 374–375)

The excesses in programming, along with the new video technology, create a television environment that abounds in entertainment and information alternatives. Shortly after Powers's book appeared in 1990, the movie "Home Alone" came out. *USA Today* asked some third-graders how they would spend unsupervised time if they had the chance. One nine-year-old knew exactly what he wanted to do: "I'd watch triple-X videos and HBO." Without making too much of one child's unchildish remark, there is something profoundly sad behind his words. Embedded in them you see not only the loss of youthful innocence but adult-oriented cues directly from television. The medium does more than entertain.

Viewed metaphorically, it is useful to imagine the different forms of media as being both windows and mirrors. Through them we not only learn about aspects of life, but we also receive reflections back—what the creators of popular culture interpret as our attitudes and traits. Today, with so many messages available, overcrowding occurs within the popular culture. People jostling in this dollar-driven environment try different approaches to stand apart, as they keep asking themselves: How can we slice through the media clutter to gain the attention of *a* public, if not *the* public as a whole? Fear of ho-hum similarity often breeds the shocking and outrageous, because the shocking and outrageous always seem to draw a crowd of some size.

On television, at the movies, and over radio or musical sound systems of whatever size, you can see and hear just about anything—the good, the bad, the ugly, and everything in between. With so many media outlets and sources, each taste gets served, whether you prefer (these options are highly selective) old movies, current events, new music videos, all sports, or nonstop comedy. However, given so much choice, being different to an extreme helps in becoming distinctive. Shock value means market share, and this is why "the cutting edge" is now no more than a momentary line in ever-shifting sand. Television talk shows devolve into raucous slugfests. Movies perfect the depiction of human dismemberment and death. Stand-up comedians build whole routines around four-letter words and bodily functions. Rap music turns more brutally violent, producing the new offshoot "gangsta rap" and a climate that culminated in the murder of two performers, Tupac Shakur and Notorious B.I.G.

The front page of the April 6, 1998 edition of the *New York Times* featured an article by Lawrie Mifflin under the headline "TV Stretches Limits of Taste, to Little Outcry." The first two paragraphs set the tone for a detailed examination of one medium in what is later referred to as a "culture, which has grown more permissive":

> Like a child acting outrageously naughty to see how far he can push his parents, mainstream television this season is flaunting the most vulgar and explicit sex, language and behavior that it has ever sent into American homes. And as sometimes happens with the spoiled child, the tactic works: attention is being paid.
>
> Ratings are high, few advertisers are rebelling against even the most provocative shows, and more and more parents seem

to have given up resisting their children in squabbles over television. Often, in a nation of two-income families and single parents, children are left alone to watch whatever they want.

Outrages of excess and acts of what normally would be considered highly questionable behavior are now common fare on "mainstream television," with the young in countless instances "left alone to watch whatever they want." In 1998, this meant (among other things) *The Jerry Springer Show*, which in one April week that year provided programs with the following titles: "Dumped for Another Woman," "Torn between Two Lovers," "My Daughter Is a Teen Prostitute," "I'm Pregnant by My Brother," and "I'm in a Bizarre Love Triangle." Besides the ratings success of this syndicated program, 1998 also brought the Comedy Central cartoon series *South Park* to the status of the most popular show on cable television. *South Park* features third-graders who speak like steaming stevedores, share ethnic, racist, and sexist jokes, and break wind with shameless abandon. Much "more scatological than logical" in the phrase of one commentator, the adult cartoon also includes gay pets, talking fecal matter, and a character who keeps dying in episode after episode. In short, *The Simpsons* and even MTV's *Beavis and Butthead* seem less daring with what *South Park* is now doing.

Beyond the ever vaster, and violent, and vulgar wasteland of television lies a popular culture landscape that makes the world of just a decade ago look curiously tame in comparison. Movie reviews—like war dispatches—now include body counts, and certain celluloid scenes that push "special effects" to sense-numbing, state-of-the-art grotesquery might make an emergency room staff cringe. Sensation supplants story, with what film makers call "graphic realism" closer to gory surrealism. As Norman Corwin observes in *Trivializing America: The Triumph of Mediocrity*, " . . . it is a curious notion that in order to escape from tensions created by daily increments of brutality, killings and terror, we go to see films of brutality, killings and terror."

Granted we are dealing with make-believe and the actors involved in sanguinary stunts rarely suffer lasting ill-effects; however, one wonders about the consequences of all the cinematic carnage on the culture and our society. Ads promoting Oliver Stone's 1994 production, *Natural Born Killers,* promised "delirious, daredevil fun." This madcap adventure, the leading box-office hit for weeks, included the showing of almost a hundred killings in horrifying, bullets-in-the-face, throat-slashing detail. Whose "fun" is this?

In her book *Mayhem: Violence as Public Entertainment,* the moral philosopher Sissela Bok examines the contemporary environment and probes whether television and movie violence provide "harmless amusement" or something else. She finds a definite correlation between violence in the media and the world as it is. Especially for the young without a wide variety of reference points, there can be a series of negative effects from violent fare: "increased fearfulness, progressive desensitization, greater appetite for more frequent and more violent programming, and higher levels of aggression." As noted before, products of popular culture exist in large measure to meet demands of people doing business in a busy marketplace. Bok favors exerting economic pressure on the creators, distributors, and advertisers of "carnage as entertainment." But as long as there is paying audience, there will be new, ever more sophisticated techniques to portray injury and death with excruciating care and verisimilitude.

Moviegoers queasy about portrayals of violence will also find that comedies keep pushing in the direction of scenes that startle and jolt—and often offend. The opening sentences of the *New York Times* July 15, 1998 review of the summer 1998 box-office hit *There's Something About Mary* dance on a razor's edge: "Sometimes Western civilization declines in deliriously funny style. Why bother to list the myriad offenses given by 'There's Something About Mary,' the proudly obnoxious new film by Peter and Bobby Farrelly, when it's easier—definitely much too easy—to enjoy them? In the raunchy wake of 'Dumb and Dumber' and 'Kingpin,' the Farrelly brothers have made a romantic comedy that's a hoot in every sense, worth a smidgen of disapproval and a whole lot of helpless laughter." Blurbs in the movie's ads carried such lines as "Pushes the envelope like you've never seen before" and "You won't believe what the Farrelly brothers got away with." Each envelope that gets pushed today moves Hollywood to try something even more outrageous the next time—and on, and on. You get the picture.

As taboos turn into anachronisms, language becomes more profane, sex more explicit, violence more brutal. Something that is off-limits today can be passé tomorrow, with the pop culture spiral similar to an oil drill boring downward for the deposit that promises the most profitable exploitation. Locating this type of American crude might be rewarding for some, but there are worrisome consequences that extend beyond anyone's concept of entertainment.

Increasingly, it has become difficult to avoid the media's messages and their impact across the culture at large. Prior to the 1996 presidential election, Republican candidate Bob Dole went to Hollywood to complain about the "nightmares of depravity" emanating from the California studios. Producer Norman Lear, who helped change the content of prime-time television in the 1970s with such programs as *All in the Family* and *Maude,* shot back with a legitimate question: "How different is the excess of violence in films and television from the excess of violence in campaigning, where in every race across the country, the campaign issues are used to destroy another human being?" Whether entertainment or politics, similar media values operate, affecting how to arrest the attention of people who are constantly bombarded with messages of all kind.

In a related realm, journalistic coverage of sensational stories that involve well-known figures—O. J. Simpson's arrest for murder and subsequent trials, Princess Diana's fatal car accident, President Bill Clinton's sexual appetites and their consequences—become consuming obsessions in contemporary communications, particularly television. Informing the public seems to take a back seat to reporting and speculating that do little more than keep a story about a prominent person alive. Before too long news gives way to pseudo news as what seem to be tangential or even trivial matters receive intensive attention.

The multimedia frenzies produce overload and overkill—and

trivialization through excess. When one story becomes the only story for some outlets, is the public being responsibly served? Unfortunately, until producers and editors think beyond the four-sided news box of sex, violence, conflict, and celebrity, Americans can expect spectacles, such as the Simpson and Clinton cases, to be continuing narratives of our popular culture. Although the new media environment deserves new definitions of news and less predictable approaches to subjects, competition and the mania for audience drive journalistic thinking and stifle beyond-the-box creativity.

The affair/crisis/scandal involving President Clinton and former White House intern Monica Lewinsky, which the public first heard about in January 1998, is a textbook example of how far contemporary media will go in covering one story. To be sure, having an incumbent president under scrutiny for adulterous conduct and sustained machinations to cover it up has a five-alarm urgency for news people—and it is legitimate as a subject. Early on, however, any sense of proportionality got lost in a headlong rush for any scrap of new information or a novel angle of interpretation.

The principle of "less is more" does not operate in such circumstances, and whole programs revolve around the latest detail or item of speculation. All-news television operations—CNN, CNBC, MSNBC, and Fox News—dramatically increased their viewership by devoting endless hours to the story. For example, *The Big Show* on MSNBC had its audience grow from 80,000 pre-Monica to 219,000 following the revelations. With so many new watchers, MSNBC was reluctant to switch subjects away from what it nightly billed as "White House in Crisis." Interestingly, though, MSNBC's prime-time host Keith Olbermann articulated his own ethical doubts in a lecture at his alma mater, Cornell University. In the spring of 1998, before the president admitted anything, Olbermann confessed: "I'm having the dry heaves in the bathroom because my moral sensor is going off, but I can't even hear it; I'm so seduced by these ratings that I go along with them when they say do this not just one hour a night but two." Eventually, Olbermann had sufficient qualms about the daily emphasis on the one story that he left the network on December 4, 1998, almost a full year into the "crisis." His valedictory statement, an op-ed column in the *New York Times* (December 8, 1998), carried the headline "The Scandal That Ate My TV Program."

When President Clinton finally acknowledged his involvement with Monica Lewinsky (on August 17, 1998) and Independent Counsel Kenneth Starr released his report about the president's actions and attempts at concealment (on September 11, 1998), it was impossible to avoid what most people traditionally have termed "private matters." Clinical linguistic precision of the so-called "Starr Report" received such amplification throughout journalism that James Naughton, the president of the Poynter Institute for Media Studies, remarked: "The question today is whether there are any taste barriers left at all." Larry Flynt, the publisher of *Hustler* magazine, used irony to compliment the seemingly over-zealous Starr: "You have opened a new era in promoting explicit sexual materials."

And where had this whole squalid saga taken America? On the *Newsweek* cover for September 28, 1998, the question "How Low Can It Go?" runs above a mock front-page of a supermarket tabloid. Every story of "The Starr" relates to the "D.C. SEX WAR!" Inside, the article by Howard Fineman and Mark Hosenball cogently captures the times and the theme of excess:

> The machinery of politics feels stuck in overdrive. Every trend in our public life since the Beatles arrived has been driven to a destructive extreme—and all the trends are converging on Clinton. Politicians who learned the clever use of polls and TV have forgotten—if they ever knew—how to talk honestly, and voters know it. Criminal investigations, once rare and therefore sobering, are now so common that they have taken over politics entirely. Spin doctors who absorbed the political skill and stagecraft of Kennedy and Reagan have never bothered with ideology, and are now too dizzy with "spin" to think straight, or seriously, about anything. The media, driven by ratings, are no less confused. The competition grows ever more fierce for

an ever-smaller audience—and so the tastes of political junkies who watch cable TV dictate the whole industry's news coverage.

The consequences of what we see and hear across the media affect not only the audience (of whatever size) but the people making news. As the impeachment inquiry of President Clinton for his conduct in the Lewinsky imbroglio began, one member of the House of Representatives withheld his response to another in their judiciary committee meeting because the two were scheduled to appear together on a television program that evening, and he did not want—in his words—"to ruin the show tonight." Television requires sparks, so why burn off your best lines in a governmental or official setting? That something strangely convoluted is taking place suggests how transforming our media culture can be. The cart can come before the horse, if the cart carries the necessary communications equipment.

In *The Argument Culture: Moving from Debate to Dialogue,* Deborah Tannen defines our time as a succession of shouting matches and running feuds. Polarized contention, featuring criticism and aggression, pits one view (often of the most extreme perspective) against another. Focusing on the media, politics, the law, and education, Tannen effectively explains how an environment of all-argument all-the-time can affect not only the argumentative participants in such a culture but the wider culture itself. She makes a telling point about journalism's connection to citizenship and "a sense of community":

> The increasingly adversarial spirit of our contemporary lives is fundamentally related to a phenomenon that has been much remarked upon in recent years: the breakdown of a sense of community. In this spirit, distinguished journalist and author Orville Schell points out that in his day journalists routinely based their writing on a sense of connection to their subjects—and that this sense of connection is missing from much that is written by journalists today. Quite the contrary, a spirit of demonography often prevails that has just the opposite effect: Far from encouraging us to feel connected to the subjects, it encourages us to feel critical, superior—and, as a result, distanced.

The cumulative effect is that citizens feel more and more cut off
from the people in public life they read about. (p. 24)

Although the news media emphasize conflict in portraying
American political life, our two-party system and checks-and-
balances governmental structure tend to push most politicians to
centrist ground, where consensus and compromise become possible. Freedom fosters fringe groups and figures of every possible
viewpoint, as Lyman Tower Sargent's anthology *Extremism in
America: A Reader* comprehensively and disturbingly shows. Yet
for those unwilling to participate in either of the major parties
gaining a political following of any consequence is difficult—and
in most cases impossible. Ross Perot's collection of nearly 20
million votes (19 percent) in 1992 was, indeed, remarkable; however, like former president Theodore Roosevelt's third-party
showing of over 4 million votes (27.4 percent) in the presidential campaign of 1912, the support was less extremist than dis-
enchanted centrist. In both cases, the national candidates for
the Democrats and Republicans seemed wanting, with vivid alternatives coming to the fore with insurgent yet mainstream
popularity.

Despite the institutional centrism of practical, elective politics, it is not hard to see the going to extremes within government. Franklin Roosevelt's New Deal in the 1930s set in motion
an activist federal government with a more prominent role in the
lives of all Americans. As certain initiatives and programs took
root and flowered, they grew to become more encompassing—
and different from how they were first envisioned. Passage in
1935 of the Social Security Act, which included Aid to Families with Dependent Children, demonstrated a necessary and be-
nevolent compassion, but also over time helped create a culture
of entitlement. In subsequent years and with the establishment
of Medicare, Medicaid, and other programs, the federal treasury
resembled a bursar's office for people receiving entitlements. For
fiscal year 1996, the largest outlay of the government ($597 bil-
lion or 37 percent of the budget) funded Social Security, Medicare, and other retirement services, according to the Internal

Revenue Service. An additional $287 billion (18 percent) went to Medicaid, food stamps, AFDC, and other social programs.

As government expanded and served new functions in people's lives, other possibilities—based on good intentions, of course—were proposed and enacted. Each measure came with costs and consequences that were either not known or predicted. As Theodore H. White explains in *America in Search of Itself*, "All entitlement programs tend not only to grow in cost, but, more important, to create their own constituencies. In 1956, Congress passed a disability insurance amendment to Social Security, estimating it would rise in cost to $860 million by 1980. By 1980, it cost more than $15 billion a year. In 1977, to cite an extreme example, a minor amendment to the Small Business Administration's act made farmers eligible for disaster loans. The cost that year was estimated at $20 million dollars; it turned out to be $1.4 billion." Such growth eventually led to an awareness of the need for greater accountability and limits to public largesse.

In addition to the explosion in entitlements, Cold War insecurity about a potential superpower battle with the Soviet Union resulted in a continuing (as well as expensive) build-up of sophisticated weaponry. Even before the Vietnam War and the marked increase in military spending during Ronald Reagan's years as president, Max Lerner titled a study of Cold War tension *The Age of Overkill*. The concept of overkill—with missile systems and other armaments able to destroy earthly civilization everywhere not merely once (which would be sufficient) but multiple times—is yet another example of going to excess. (Before the Gulf War in 1991, it was widely reported that the U.S. had enough chemical weapons to destroy the world's population approximately five thousand times.) Now, with the demise of the Soviet Union, there is the new worry about what to do with all of the existing *matériel*.

Although in rhetorical terms Ronald Reagan preached the virtues of smaller, less expensive government, his policies never matched his words. Defense spending during the 1980s, along with the continuation of most domestic programs, resulted in persistent deficits and a gargantuan federal debt. It would take

Bill Clinton, a Democratic president forced to the center by a Republican-controlled Congress, to re-examine or change several entitlement programs, including Aid to Families with Dependent Children. In 1996, Temporary Assistance for Needy Families replaced AFDC and shifted responsibility for poor families to the states. Controversial as these actions became, they recognized that closer supervision and stricter time limits to receive support might help control the growth and costs. Initiatives of this kind sought a new meaning of governmental responsibility and the bases for entitlement.

In recent years, too, the legal system has faced challenges that test the boundaries of what could be considered permissible action, of how far to carry anyone's claim of justice. From what the public knew of certain cases, criminals seemed to enjoy better treatment than their victims. In an essay to celebrate the 200th anniversary of the Bill of Rights in 1991, Max Lerner pursued his idea of "overkill" from a different direction. The province of rights, from his perspective, needed careful and constant monitoring to avoid the going to extremes:

> the achievements of the culture of freedoms should not blind us to the dangers it faces. One is the danger of turning the Bill of Rights into a fortress of absolutism. Every successful idea, at some point, becomes excessive and rigid. There are ominous signs that our procedural safeguards have come to care more for the wrong-doer than for his victims—that in seeking protection for freedoms we may be abandoning the need of every culture for limits. Abstract rights ought not to be pushed ahead of the safety and well-meaning of real people.
>
> My own fighting faith, two centuries into the history of the Bill of Rights, is that our task in the next century will be to find a synthesis within our own minds, between freedoms, rights and limits.

Seeking a realistic and workable synthesis between freedoms and limits—or an appropriate middle ground between extremes of a condition or situation—is critical to tempering excesses of the kind we have experienced in our past and what we see around us today. There is something absurd about the frenzy for money in collegiate sports, which often subordinates the student

status of these amateur athletes. Academic progress and gradu-
ation rates—in short, the education process and why schools exist—receive less emphasis than they deserve at many institutions,
with a disproportionate tail wagging the dog itself. Moreover, at
many of the same schools where athletics raise questions and
problems, the emphasis on faculty publication—the publish-or-
perish syndrome—often undercuts accomplishment in the classroom. As one academic cracked about a highly specialized col-
league, "He's exactly what this university wants today—the
author of one unreadable book a year."

In the corporate world in 1998, the average compensation for
chief executive officers rose 36 percent, while the increase for
the American workforce overall was 2.7 percent. The CEOs at
major U.S. companies in 1998 earned 419 times the pay of their
average workers. Will such disparity ultimately lead to lasting
economic divisions that threaten not only those who try to get
by day-to-day but people in the stabilizing, shoulder-to-the-
wheel middle class that has been fundamental to this country's
development? That the top 1 percent of Americans have more
wealth than the bottom 90 percent, according to a 1998 study, is
as much cause for alarm as the mounting number of personal
bankruptcies in the United States—1.3 million in 1997, which is
more than double the figure of a decade ago. Such economic extremes, along with what have become regularly announced em-
ployee cutbacks at many large companies, draw into question the
happy-go-lucky prosperity that has been celebrated during the
late 1990s.

The seemingly endless pursuit of campaign money by politicians signifies a system spinning in an orbit far removed from
the borders of reason. President Clinton's appetite for so-called
"soft money" to advance his re-election in 1996 dramatizes a de-
meaning process that forces candidates for high office to devote
hour-after-hour hunting for contributions that often raise more
questions than civic concerns. Like the arms race of Cold War
days, politicians believe a bigger war chest is a better war chest,
and insecurity drives them to collect ever greater amounts and
to exploit any loophole. Whether such devotion is in the public
interest can be assessed by gauging the skepticism with which

Americans regard public figures today and by noting the critical portrayals of politics in several Hollywood films, like *Wag the Dog, Primary Colors,* and *Bulworth*—all of which appeared within months of each other in 1998. Waging what has become a "permanent campaign" to have ready money for any political eventuality makes government service more difficult. Campaign fundraising never really stops—and neither do the doubts about what all those dollars are buying.

In their seminal 1890 *Harvard Law Review* article on privacy, future Supreme Court Justice Louis Brandeis and Samuel Warren argued that "the right to be let alone" was fundamental in America, noting "the common law secures to each individual the right of determining . . . to what extent his thoughts, sentiments, and emotions shall be communicated to others." In recent decades and for a panoply of reasons, any notion of privacy seems a quaint anachronism rather than an American right. The post-Watergate ethos of journalism tore down many of the previous boundaries that existed between what was considered legitimate for coverage and what the public did not need to know about a person in the news. Certainly some of the reporting in this tell-all environment is justified—we should know, for example, whether a president leads a reckless private life—but do we need microscopic attention directed to every wart on someone's anatomy? Beyond journalism, contemporary biographies now show little reluctance to chronicle vice and villainy, whether the subject be John F. Kennedy, Lyndon Johnson, Nancy Reagan, Elizabeth Taylor, Tennessee Williams, F. Scott Fitzgerald, or Leonard Bernstein. Joyce Carol Oates's apt term for this burgeoning genre is "pathography," and such work is as out of proportion as the holy-card hagiography of earlier times. To make every private moment a matter of public consumption can cheapen life itself, and it serves no higher purpose than mass-marketed voyeurism.

To discuss other contemporary examples could, alas, become excessive, the academic equivalent to an "X Game," with the "X" shorthand for—what else?—"extreme." So a metaphor might help provide resolution. In many of the different areas being examined, what at first appears to be the deliberate motion of a pendulum increases speed, resulting in wildly rapid swings that seem simultaneous and contradictory, when, in effect, the original arc of action has created an opposite reaction—with both action and reaction existing at the same time. Viewed another way, it is as though a thesis *and* an antithesis form directly from the original idea, with the synthesis getting lost in the process. As the next essay argues, modern-day America is simultaneously experiencing a time of acute sensitivity and astonishing shock. Oftentimes, though, these two opposing extremes provoke tensions that are either left unresolved or resolved by reactions that themselves seem even more extreme.

Keeping the country on an even keel, in a state of relative equilibrium, at its level best, reduces the possibility of the dangerous consequences that come from the clash of countervailing forces. To lose sight of first intentions or objectives is to run the risk of going too far in ways that ultimately undermine those intentions or objectives. When freedom trumps other values and turns into license, equality suffers and extremism (of one kind or another) flourishes. American history and what is happening today offer continuing lessons in liberties indecently taken, making it difficult, if not impossible, to achieve the nation's founding goal of "a more perfect Union."

THE UNSETTLING OF AMERICA

When the Christopher Columbus Quincentenary Commission was created in 1984, Congress envisioned a national celebration in 1992 marking the triumphant discovery of "the new world" in 1492. In the intervening eight years, however, America changed. By 1992 and the years that followed, controversy surrounded any observance of Columbus and his voyage.

Welcome to the new America that is now remarkably unsettled about its past, present, and future.

The continuing debate over Columbus illustrates the political and cultural forces pulling America in opposite directions—and away from anything resembling a strong, vibrant center of common thinking and belief. In the case of Columbus, people wanting a patriotic pageant sailed into the rocky waters of those who blame the explorer for setting in motion (in the words of the American Library Association) "cultural imperialism, colonialism and the Native-American holocaust." So many newspaper and magazine accounts of the quincentenary quarrel carried the headline "Goodbye, Columbus" that the phrase quickly became trite.

Bidding farewell to some figure's heroic stature is nothing new. In the tell-all environment of the past three decades, few living or deceased public figures have escaped the disclosure of telltale information pointing out their clay feet or other body parts. But what is striking about contemporary America is the rampant revisionism taking place. Once commonly accepted national principles and ideals now face constant challenges. Just

34

look around. Everything seems up for grabs. There are few areas of life that do not provoke argument. People of opposing viewpoints embrace extreme positions. Problems fester and multiply in an atmosphere fostering acrimony rather than resolution.

This unsettling of America is in part a consequence of new thinking about the role of groups in our country. Historically, individualism (or what Emerson called "self-reliance") stood out as a dominant trait of the national character. Then along came the multiple social revolutions of the 1960s and 1970s, with their calls for civil rights, women's rights, gay rights, gray rights, and all the rest.

The result today is much more emphasis on what an organized group can achieve. Whether united by race, ethnicity, gender, religion, or sexual orientation, strength comes from numbers. That strength takes different forms—collective identity, information distribution, political lobbying. By being visible and vocal, groups assert themselves, make their grievances known, and propose measures to improve their political and social standing.

Enhancing human dignity and righting wrongs to obtain greater equality of opportunity are admirable objectives for any group to pursue. Yet, increasingly, working toward such goals is carrying people to extremes and eroding common ground between the group and the larger national community. A singular interest thus threatens the broader public interest, with one consequence being more and more fragmentation.

As groups gain influence, they begin to flex their collective muscle. As a result, Americans have become more aware of offending a person, or an entire group, by saying or doing something in conflict with the accepted thinking of, let's say, Native Americans, African-Americans, women, or homosexuals.

In fact, a name for our time might well be the Age of Sensitivity. Examples abound:

• Native Americans conduct campaigns protesting the nicknames of sports teams—the Atlanta Braves, the Cleveland

Indians, the Washington Redskins. In 1992, the *Oregonian,* the largest newspaper in Oregon, established a policy of no longer publishing these nicknames.

• At Bennington College, the noted writer Edward Hoagland was fired from his teaching position when students persuaded campus authorities that an essay he wrote for *Esquire* reflected bias against homosexuals. (Hoagland was ultimately reinstated after an investigation found the school "deviated from proper . . . procedures.")

• African-Americans in Illinois, California, and elsewhere seek to ban Mark Twain's *Adventures of Huckleberry Finn* and *The Adventures of Tom Sawyer* from school reading lists, because Huck and Tom's friend is called "Nigger Jim."

• Comedian Billy Crystal's joke at the 1990 Oscar ceremony about the Mafia and movie-making provoked Italian-American groups. Fifty-two members of Congress subsequently signed a statement charging Crystal with "soiling the reputations of . . . 26 million citizens of Italian heritage."

• The New York production of the play *Miss Saigon* was in danger of never opening on Broadway because a white male played a Eurasian role. And the Tony Award-winning musical *The Will Rogers Follies* was confronted by three protest campaigns: from women, Native Americans, and minority actors.

What's been occurring on many college or university campuses epitomizes the Age of Sensitivity. At Harvard University, a professor of history was accused of "racial insensitivity" for reading from a Southern planter's diary without also reading from a slave's account. At the University of Northern Colorado, a Hispanic woman (and former Reagan administration official) was "disinvited" as the commencement speaker when her views on affirmative action and bilingual education became known. At New York University School of Law, a hypothetical moot-court case involving the child-custody rights of a divorced lesbian mother was withdrawn because students refused to argue (or listen to) what might be interpreted as an anti-homosexual perspective.

More than reflecting the Age of Sensitivity, such incidents serve as examples of the "politically correct movement" affecting American life. In the late 1980s and 1990s, American colleges and universities responded to verbal or physical acts of discrimination by establishing codes that banned offenses directed at anyone's race, sex, ethnic origin, disability, religion, or sexual orientation. What began with the salutary goal of discouraging harassment spun out of control in several places, such as Duke, Harvard, Michigan, and Stanford. Generally across academia there is a continuing chilling effect from "politically correct" thinking that often freezes public reaction.

Such an intellectual climate breeds fear. *Newsweek* bannered a cover story about the PC movement with the phrase "Thought Police." In his syndicated column, the late America-watcher and professor Max Lerner noted that many a campus "is becoming a dark wood of monster taboos, where a teacher is judged not by the quality of his thinking and teaching but by his conformity to taboos enforced by self-appointed vigilantes of the mind."

Instead of fostering free inquiry and free speech, some colleges and universities are turning into places where anxiety about being perceived as insensitive leads to a reluctance to discuss subjects that, even in the abstract, might offend an individual or group. The extent to which hypersensitive thinking about "oppression" pervades the academic mind is captured well in a document circulated by Smith College's Office of Student Affairs. It offers a litany of "isms" to be strictly avoided:

- ABLEISM—oppression of the differently abled by the temporarily able.
- AGEISM—oppression of the young and the old by young adults and the middle-aged, in the belief that others are "incapable" or unable to take care of themselves.
- LOOKISM—the belief that appearance is an indicator of a person's value; the construction of a standard for beauty/

attractiveness; oppression through stereotypes and generalizations of both those who do not fit that standard and those who do.

To read the complete Smith College statement is to get the feeling that oppression lurks everywhere. "Lookism," for example, covers physique, hair color and length, grooming and wardrobe, among other items. In the eyes of some people, a short person now is "vertically challenged." (Saying someone has "a Napoleonic complex" is no doubt incorrect and objectionable on several grounds.)

But not even the Smith College document goes as far as the *Random House Webster's College Dictionary,* which offers "womyn" as an acceptable alternate spelling for "women." "Womyn" is permissible, according to the usage note, "to avoid the suggestion of sexism perceived in the sequence m-e-n." On some campuses, "womyn" has even become the preferred spelling.

Another affected area is the world of popular communications. Cable News Network sought to avoid the use of the word "foreign," with its possibly negative suggestion, proposing "international" instead. A *Dictionary of Cautionary Words and Phrases* is now consulted at many newspapers across the country, with journalists advised against writing sentences that include such phrases as "Dutch treat" (anti-Dutch), "siesta" (connotes Latin laziness), "gyp" (a Gypsy slur), and both "cheesecake" and "beefcake." In advertising, gone are the days when Alka-Seltzer copywriters could have an actor exclaim: "Mama Mia! That's a spicy meatball!"

Doing anything that might be interpreted as offensive—or even stereotypical—is now risky. Beer commercials, which are primarily aimed at younger males, still feature festive females in bouncy beach scenes, but these spots face growing criticism and even lawsuits. Some advertisers refuse to show people at all to avoid offending any segment of the public. Comical croaking frogs prove safer.

Being sensitive to another's feelings is one thing—a legacy of the humanistic tradition and religious principles of any faith known to God (or, lest I insult believers in other deities, to any nameless nondenominational higher being). But hypersensitivity is another matter, inviting ridicule and interfering with understanding between people. To be scared of the potential consequences of tribalization, balkanization, or polarization might be linguistically offensive to Native Americans, Balkans, or Eskimos. However, it is becoming a genuine fear.

At a time when one hears increasingly about the "cultural diversity" of America, it makes little sense to create barriers in thinking, language, and action that ultimately could end up isolating one person from another or one group from another. Without some set of common values and beliefs, a country can become floating islands frequently colliding in open water.

Incongruously, even paradoxically, all this concern over sensitivity is occurring at a moment when we are being told that the public has become "desensitized" to several realms of reality: namely, violence, sex, and crime. In fact, to cast an eye in the direction of our popular culture (which, to a certain degree, reflects the many dimensions of the public mind at a given time) makes one think this is, indeed, an Age of Shock rather than an Age of Sensitivity. A few examples:

- Bret Easton Ellis's novel *American Psycho* describes in horrific detail the torture and murder of women—and becomes a best seller. Another novel, *Vox* by Nicholson Baker, achieves similar status by documenting the possibilities of telephonic sex.
- The movie *The Silence of the Lambs* features the aptly named character "Hannibal the Cannibal." Audiences find his behavior eerily engrossing, and the movie (about catching a serial killer) wins five Oscars, including one for Best Picture.
- Battling to retain viewers and achieve higher ratings, television executives have decided that sex might be the magic bullet. Critic John J. O'Conner noted in the *New York Times*, "There's hardly an hour on network entertainment schedules these days without sexual reverberations." Shock-radio, too, has found its niche locally and nationally.

- Modern music includes such genres as "death metal" (the group Cannibal Corpse has a popular album called *Butchered at Birth*) and "radical rap" (Ice Cube's *Death Certificate* dwells on racial strife, women as sex objects, and violence).
- In contemporary comedy, some performers (notably Andrew Dice Clay and the late Sam Kinison) build routines around fullthroated outbursts directed at women, minorities, homosexuals, new immigrants, the homeless, the handicapped and other groups. Any sense of playfulness is overwhelmed by an unrelenting tone of anger and hatred.

The primary audience for much of this fare is college-age men and women who are simultaneously, of course, being influenced by the "politically correct" movement. Caught between extremes there's no real middle ground for young people, and they find it difficult to resolve conflicting signals coming from two shaping forces in their lives: the educational establishment and the pop culture world of the media.

What do the extreme responses of sensitivity and shock tell us about ourselves? In the abstract, politically correct thinking took root in the rich American soil of freedom, fairness, equality, tolerance, and compassion. In practice, many PC crusaders turn these virtues upside down, inverting meaning in Orwellian ways. Going to extremes trivializes the cause, no matter how worthy the original motivation and purpose.

As for the shocking messages that surround us, they are products of a post-1960s communications environment that pushes free expression beyond previous limits. As creative people of all kinds go further and further, they discover that the most outrageous, bizarre, and extreme statements or actions get attention. In a cut-throat competitive climate, where the promise of multimillion dollar deals is the reward for blockbuster success, an attitude of "we can top that" is inevitable—and it will persist until the consuming audience says "enough is enough."

Sensational elements pervade books, films, television programs, and musical works because the creators see such elements as eye-opening, sometimes throat-grabbing responses to legitimate subjects and serious concerns of contemporary American life. Racial conflict, random (and gruesome) violence, economic disparity between the haves and have-nots, debilitation from drugs, sexual promiscuity among teens and young adults do exist—and don't succumb to romanticized renderings. Treating such topics often leads writers and performers to "heighten the reality," making the portrayal even more compelling.

In doing this, of course, the shocking becomes even more so. What once might have possessed "shock value" no longer does—and the technology to create special film and television effects is now so sophisticated there seems to be an ongoing battle in Hollywood to produce works that glorify mayhem and gore. In this environment, nothing is suggestive or subtle. Danger has little time to lurk, as one goosebump-raising scene follows another.

Increasingly, Americans seem of two minds when confronted by sensational stimuli, especially involving violence. The reactions of dread and fascination compete; our fear of being the victim of violent crime grows daily, yet we flock to "action" movies featuring exploding heads. You can say, quite rightly, "That's entertainment." However, the live television and radio coverage of the trial of serial killer Jeffrey Dahmer in Milwaukee in 1992 drew a considerable audience. Listeners learned in gruesome detail about dismembering bodies, storing human hearts in the freezer, and boiling a victim's head before removing the skin and painting the skull.

Americans, of course, are no strangers to violence. Carving a civilization out of the wilderness frontier and fighting wars across the globe make our heritage more bloodstained than we usually care to admit. Today, though, our absorption in violence seems much different from such former justifications as having "a job to do" or "a cause to fight for."

The vivid portrayal of violence directed at huge audiences now serves, ironically, as a release from pent-up fear about real violence. It is almost as though we are afraid of a violent, unknown, modern wilderness out there on the streets that is overtaking civilization itself. Vicariously experiencing violence in the controlled environment of our homes or neighborhood theaters becomes cathartic, a way of coping with the physical and psychological threats that we perceive surround us.

It is chancy, though, to offer too many generalizations about a territory as vast and varied as popular culture. With such abundance, almost anything you say about it is true. Just as the shocking stands out, so too does sensitivity. On television, for example, a professor of psychiatry at the Harvard Medical School reviewed scripts of *The Cosby Show* for years to be sure there was no suggestion of prejudice or insensitive stereotyping. A movie like Kevin Costner's *Dances with Wolves* depicts Native Americans as noble inhabitants of the post–Civil War West who suffered abject mistreatment by whites. The arresting fable by Barry Lopez about a journey through the North American wilderness, *Crow and Weasel,* occupied best-seller lists in late 1990 and early 1991; the author's note points out that the book is "set in myth time and written with respect for Native American values and oral traditions."

Interestingly, *Dances with Wolves* and *Crow and Weasel* are popular works that reflect America's newfound willingness to look at the West as something more than John Wayne territory. They dramatize the Native American experience so appealingly that the response is, in part, paleface guilt. That's one reason why the controversy over observing the Columbus Quincentenary proved to be as much a reflection of our times as it was an occasion to recall what took place 500 years ago.

The pendulum has swung from one mythic extreme to another. And instead of making an effort to find a reasonable common ground that recognizes both the good and the bad, many historians and cultural commentators remain fixed at one pole or the other. In this environment, academic organizations have had to become balancing routines. For example, the American Studies Association called its 1992 annual meeting "Exploration/Exploitation: The Americas," with sessions devoted to "the finding/invention/conquest of America." Strategic wording and punctuation are required these days.

No one can deny the value of continuing analysis and reappraisal of what has happened or might be occurring in the life of a people. Nothing should be sacred or out of bounds in coming to terms with the past or present in a realistic, fair, and comprehensive way. A danger arises, however, when the thinking or action gets carried to such extremes that reasoned, nuanced understanding is sacrificed.

Some observers of America today go so far as to say that there is "culture war" raging in this country, though the metaphor of war might be yet another example of the shocking phrase chosen to grab attention. Clearly, we see political and cultural conflict, but that conflict—between sensitivity and shock, between traditional historical interpretations and rampant revisionism, between believers in the mythic "dream" and the decline-minded—invigorates public discourse and provokes back-to-basics questioning.

Just as clearly, there is embedded in the conflict a destructive element. Going to extremes is not new in America; what is distinctive about this particular time is the number of extreme viewpoints competing for attention and acceptance. Even in elective politics you see an ominous trend of accentuating what are called "wedge issues" to drive people apart. Negative campaigning, with stark or shocking messages on television and radio, becomes a perfect vehicle for dividing rather than uniting.

Unity created by fostering shared, core beliefs no longer seems a primary concern. The center has trouble holding because the most vocal and visible forces animate the polar positions. Lincoln's sobering and often-repeated warning that a "house divided against itself cannot stand" may have possessed greater pertinence during the days before the Civil War, but the compelling image remains pertinent in an Age of Sensitivity *and* an Age of Shock.

Postscript

The summer 1992 issue of *Notre Dame Magazine* devoted five articles to its cover subject, "Wasteland Revisited," with "The Unsettling of America" a broader than the state-of-television view of contemporary culture. The essay grew out of a column I wrote for the *Chicago Tribune* in late 1991 about the difficulty of teaching a course about American humor at a time of acute sensitivity.

In the column, I described

> a growing reluctance to respond to humor in the public setting of a classroom out of fear that any exercise of one's funny bone will be misinterpreted. To laugh with Mark Twain at some of the shenanigans of Huckleberry Finn and Nigger Jim might be disrespectful of a former slave and his people. To be amused at the number of people from a specific ethnic group it takes to change a light bulb might be offensive to members of whatever group is named. And so on.
>
> It used to be different. Students seemed willing to accept that humor, by its nature, usually comes at someone's expense. A punch line had its own force—of provoking laughter or thought, approval or disapproval. Today it's stony, solemn silence, a hesitancy even to discuss the motivation behind a joke or the stereotyping involved.
>
> This unwillingness to respond to humor is more a sign of the times than a suggestion that young people today are a humorless lot. Where I teach isn't a hotbed of the PC movement, but the chilling effect coming from the widespread politically correct thinking does freeze public reaction.
>
> Nationally, in fact, some schools now have codes banning "inappropriately directed laughter" and the telling of certain kinds of jokes.
>
> But outside the classroom it's another story. Away from a formal setting, many students find the likes of Eddie Murphy, Andrew Dice Clay, and Sam Kinison uproariously funny. These comedians build their acts on outrageous outbursts. With routines revolving around women, minorities, gays, new immigrants, the homeless, and the handicapped, such performers are the furthest thing from hypersensitive, politically correct thinking and expression.
>
> Students today are caught in a crossfire of competing cultural movements. One force (principally the academic Establishment) pulls them in the direction of sensitivity. The other

force (largely popular culture) jerks them toward the shocking or sensational. There's no middle ground.

A teacher comes to understand the silence and sidelong glances in the classroom. It's risky to laugh if sensitivities might be violated. But privately—back in dorm rooms listening to tapes, or at movie theaters or comedy clubs—what's outlandishly crude or questionable, or both, becomes not only a source of entertainment but research material for academic essays.

Last semester, when a student handed in his major project of the term, he proudly said, "I liked doing that paper more than any other I've done, but don't show it around." It was about Andrew Dice Clay.

The pleasure dome of free inquiry known as academe is not immune from the pathogens that produce fads and fashions. Indeed, such pathogens tend to thrive in such an experimental environment, mutating rapidly and becoming more virulent as the fad or fashion gains wider recognition. Such was the case with political correctness in the early 1990s. All of a sudden, it seemed, everyone was talking about or reacting to this "movement" that really was not a movement in any traditional meaning of that word.

As laudable as many of the politically correct objectives are— respecting men, women, and children of every race, ethnicity, religion, class, sexual orientation, and physical or mental circumstance—the excesses or extremes of such thinking have become more and more troubling. To be sensitive is one thing. To find offense at every turn and to create a climate of fear that stifles expression is something else entirely. Freedom can be carried too far, as the first chapter explains; however, the opposite of freedom—call it tyranny or oppression, if you will—is *not* the appropriate response or reaction. The same is true for sensitivity. What truly shocks is the other extreme altogether.

Although the subject of political correctness no longer receives the sustained scrutiny it did a few years ago—so it goes with fads and fashions—the thinking that gave rise to the hypersensitivity of this movement persists, especially on college campuses. In 1996 at Emory and Henry College in Virginia, there was much debate and controversy over the school's nickname, the Wasps. Some students and faculty members feared that to be known as a Wasp might—instead of an insect—imply a White Anglo-Saxon Protestant (a WASP), with connotations of racial and religious superiority. The college's administration decided to keep the nickname, but make sure there is no misinterpretation.

Central to any consideration of the pros and cons of political correctness as an ideology is the more complicated subject of multiculturalism—to which we now turn.

AMERICA AND
MULTICULTURALISM

"[T]he test of a first-rate intelligence," remarked F. Scott Fitzgerald in *The Crack-Up,* "is the ability to hold two opposed ideas in the mind at the same time, and still retain the ability to function." For the United States today, the country's national mind faces a continuing test of opposing ideas—and there is talk of war both in the air and on the air. Books carry such titles as *Culture Wars: The Struggle to Define America; Loose Canons: Notes on the Culture Wars; Beyond the Culture Wars: How Teaching the Conflicts Can Revitalize American Education;* and *Battle of the Books: The Curriculum Debate in America.* Patrick Buchanan, the punch-in-the-nose pundit turned presidential candidate, thundered at the 1992 Republican National Convention, "There is a religious war going on in our country for the soul of America. It is a cultural war, as critical to the kind of nation we will one day be as was the Cold War itself."

Hype and hysteria aside, the "war" currently taking place is being waged on several fronts. To a considerable extent, however, the principal battle involves a fight over national self-definition. Not long ago, a cover of *Time* magazine asked, "Who Are We?" Answering that three-word question is becoming more difficult because in recent years so many new and different voices have been contributing their perspectives to what America means. As the comedian Jimmy Durante used to say, "Everybody's getting into the act." We are discovering that multiple viewpoints produce more scope but less focus; the trees seem relatively clear, yet the forest is somewhat blurry.

Arriving at an acceptable national self-definition is elusive. So, too, is finding a workable meaning for the adjective "multicultural," which is used with greater frequency to describe contemporary America. The *Oxford English Dictionary* definition of multicultural is: "Of or pertaining to a society consisting of varied cultural groups." An uncertainty of meaning comes in where to put the emphasis—on the singular ("a society") or on the plural ("varied cultural groups"). Jousting over precisely what to accentuate is at the heart of the so-called cultural war now being fought. The degree of stress also plays a critical role. To put the debate in the starkest, most polarizing terms: on one side, there are those who acknowledge America's pluralist nature but put a premium on unity; on the other side, there are those who subordinate the singular or unifying dimension to highlight the variety of experience contributing to American life.

With the end of the Cold War and the U.S. now being called "the only superpower," an observer from afar might find it strange to be reading about war within America. But to understand the present requires a retreat to the recent past. The 1960s and 1970s unleashed forces that have intensified in intervening years. The civil rights revolution and the women's movement set in motion an awareness of and concern for specific groups that subsequently encompassed efforts at recognition from people on grounds of not only race and gender but ethnicity, class, religion, sexual orientation, disability, and age. In the academy, programs in African-American studies, gender studies, ethnic studies, and gay studies came into being and altered the established humanities and social sciences curricula. In addition, affirmative action laws and other legislation attempted to right wrongs that put members of specific groups at disadvantages.

Emphasizing in one way or another particular groups, especially because of race, ethnicity, and gender, contributed to the "multicultural" thinking occurring in education and the wider world of government and commerce. At the same time this has been happening, the demographic composition of America has been dramatically changing. In the words of Ronald Takaki in his book *From Different Shores*, "The new face of America has a

Resident Population Distribution for the United States by Race and Hispanic Origin: 1980 and 1990

	1980		1990		
	Number	%	Number	%	Change
Total population	226,545,805	100.0	248,709,873	100.0	9.8
White	188,371,622	83.1	199,686,070	80.3	6.0
Black	26,495,020	11.7	29,986,060	12.1	13.2
American Indian, Eskimo or Aleut	1,420,400	0.6	1,959,234	0.8	37.9
Asian or Pacific Islander	3,500,439	1.5	7,273,662	2.9	107.8
Other race	6,758,319	3.0	9,804,847	3.9	45.1
Hispanic origin	14,608,673	6.4	22,354,059	9.0	53.0

darker hue." Consider the census statistics in the table (above) on race and origin, with the rate of growth reflected under the heading "Change."

According to the 1990 census, fifty-one cities with populations above 100,000 now have minorities in the majority, including New York, Los Angeles, Chicago, Houston, Dallas, Washington, D.C., Detroit, Cleveland, Atlanta, Miami, Baltimore, and San Francisco. If demographic trends continue, in 2050 the U.S. Census Bureau predicts:

	Number	%
Total population	382,700,000	100.00
White	201,800,000	52.7
Black	57,300,000	15.0
Native American	4,100,000	1.1
Asian	38,800,000	10.1
Hispanic	80,700,000	21.1

Along with the particularism of the group and the demographic colorizing, another phenomenon is contributing to what might be called America's dislocation from its past. For a number of reasons, large, at one time dominant, institutions are in decline, and they are struggling to redefine themselves in this new environment. For example, in politics the Democratic and Republican political parties no longer possess the clout they once did, with particular "special" or "single" interests, complete with contribution-giving "political action committees," now troublingly influential. In business, a full-service and countrywide merchandising operation, such as Sears Roebuck, receives stiff competition from more specialized retail companies. Throughout the media today, the word "mass" is rarely used because "narrowcasting" is replacing "broadcasting" and "niche" publishing is increasingly the path to publication success. Indeed, according to authoritative audience surveys, in three U.S. cities (Los Angeles, Miami, and San Antonio) Spanish language radio stations lead their markets. In short, institutions that formerly helped hold citizens together across a broad range of human experience no longer operate as unifying forces to the degree they once did. One can only speculate about what institutions might come into being in the future as the connective tissue or cement of American society.

Taking these circumstances together, does it come as a surprise why the word "diversity" instead of the word "unity" crops up so frequently today in conversation and in print? In his January 26, 1993 column, "In Tribal Solitude," Russell Baker of the *New York Times* played with the concept of "diversity":

Diversity:
  I am a European-American.
  I am a male European-American.
  I am a Depression-generation, male European-American.
  I am a hearing-impaired, Depression-generation, male
    European-American.
  I am a college-educated, hearing-impaired, Depression-
    generation, male European-American.

> Because I have not lost significant amounts of hair, I am not
> a bald, college-educated, hearing-impaired, Depression-
> generation, male European-American. Instead, I am a
> comb-carrying, college-educated, hearing-impaired,
> Depression-generation, male European-American.
> I am a heterosexual, comb-carrying, college-educated,
> hearing-impaired, Depression-generation, male European-
> American.
> Because I am married I am not a single, heterosexual, comb-
> carrying, college-educated, hearing-impaired, Depression-
> generation, male European-American, and therefore I do
> not go to single bars.

He goes on to introduce his wife with her particularities, and
concludes by saying:

> The Celtic-American of female gender to which I am married
> is a high school dropout and, therefore, not unwelcome,
> but made to feel peculiar in doubles bars for genderly en-
> lightened, Celt-sensitive, politically unpredictable, com-
> paratively financially disadvantaged, square, married, het-
> erosexual, comb-carrying, college-educated, hearing-
> impaired, Depression-generation, male European-
> Americans. In short, we stay home a lot.

Baker's satire, complete with its absurdity, suggests the extremes to which some people will go in recognizing diversity.
That characteristic—of carrying an effort to an extreme—is a
principal reason why the word "multiculturalism" has taken on
derogatory or pejorative connotations. In the minds of many,
emphasizing the variety and diversity of multicultural America
can go too far, as the broader yet more unifying traits held in
common fade into the background or receive outright rejection.
A note of caution, however: Baker's profession and the media in
general revel in the abnormal and magnify difference. Amid all
the coverage of disputes and divisions in the early 1990s, the
Latino National Political Survey, involving nearly 3,000 interviews, revealed that more than 90 percent of the respondents
did *not* belong to any ethnic organization and did believe all citi-

zens of the United States should learn English. Achieving access to the American mainstream animated the reaction of respondents. Of course, the lesson of this and many other surveys is that leaders of causes—who make news—might not in actuality be representative of the views of the people they claim to represent.

In *The Disuniting of America: Reflections on a Multicultural Society,* Arthur M. Schlesinger, Jr., argues that the country is in danger of losing its national identity as a result of the actions of the most extreme proponents for specific groups as opposed to the whole society. Criticizing the "ethnicity rage in general and Afrocentricity in particular," Schlesinger says: "The recent apotheosis of ethnicity, black, brown, red, yellow, white, has revived the dismal prospect that in happy melting-pot days Americans thought the republic was moving safely beyond—that is, a society fragmented into ethnic groups. The cult of ethnicity exaggerates differences, intensifies resentments and antagonisms, drives ever deeper the awful wedges between races and nationalities. The endgame is self-pity and self-ghettoization." First appearing in the Whittle Communications series of books with advertising for "managers and policymakers," *The Disuniting of America* struck such a chord that it subsequently came out as a much-advertised trade offering by the New York publisher W. W. Norton and became quite popular. The slim volume, which appeared in a revised and expanded edition in 1998, is particularly penetrating in its treatment of the consequences of "the cult of ethnicity" throughout education. What is being learned and how it is being presented shape the thinking of future generations, with history becoming a "weapon" of division.

Schlesinger's book heads the list of a growing bibliography of works by "liberal" intellectuals (C. Vann Woodward, Alfred Kazin, and Irving Howe, among others) who explain how damaging cultural fragmentation can be. These thinkers and writers receive cheers of agreement from such conservatives as William Bennett, Russell Kirk, Diane Ravitch, and George Will—not to mention Rush Limbaugh—suggesting just how far certain aspects of multiculturalism have been carried. We have strange bedfellows in the "culture wars" and what the previous essay refers to as the Age of Sensitivity. Within a week's time in 1992, a newspaper reader learned that on one coast (in Connecticut) a community college would *not* be named for America's greatest author, Mark Twain, because some students considered him a racist, while on the other coast (in Washington) the state's governor dropped the title "chief of staff" for his top aide because Native Americans objected to what they perceived to be the insensitive use of the word "chief."

Any student of United States history knows that going to extremes is an American affliction, the consequence of carrying some of our freedoms too far. As this book's opening chapter explains in some detail, the impulse to excess (wretched or otherwise) is strong and deeply rooted in our national soil. In the controversy over multiculturalism, the proponents and opponents who take their viewpoints to one or the other extreme get the most attention. That, alas, is how the media operate in defining news. But now that we know what exists on either end of the spectrum, it is critical to consider the debate anew. Examining the different perspectives—everything from the Afrocentric movement to the Eurocentric desire not to make any change in the canon of Western thought—one realizes that some reasoned limits are needed for those who view multiculturalism either positively or negatively. In addition to recognizing appropriate limits, it is also important to recall Fitzgerald's remark about "the test of a first-rate intelligence" and "two opposed ideas." Ideas in opposition need not be irreconcilable. Whitman's lines in "Song of Myself" address his personal and even more his country's condition:

> Do I contradict myself?
> Very well then I contradict myself,
> (I am large, I contain multitudes.)

Since the founding of the Republic, American citizens have engaged in a number of balancing acts: between liberty and equality, between rights and responsibilities, between prosperity and justice, between nationalistic pride and democratic naysaying, between diversity and solidarity. The diversity-solidarity dilemma is, of course, different today from yesterday because of the growing concern for specific groups and because of the greater heterogeneity of the population. Those circumstances should make plain the need to look beyond the ways of thinking and acting that took shape in the past when the word "immigrant" usually meant "white" and "European" of one nationality or another. In *Multiculturalism and "The Politics of Recognition,"* the philosopher and political theorist Charles Taylor shows the connection between identity and recognition, noting at one point: "misrecognition shows not just a lack of due respect. It can inflict a grievous wound, saddling its victims with a crippling self-hatred. Due recognition is not just a courtesy we owe people. It is a vital human need." Taylor, however, creates boundaries for this "politics of recognition." He argues that for some people focusing on identity leads to "the politics of difference," where "what we are asked to recognize is the unique identity of this individual or group, their distinctness from everyone else." In many cases, "the politics of difference" is closer to what you might call a politics of resentment. Grievances, sometimes generations old, influence thought and behavior to the point where what happened yesterday dominates today and tomorrow. Being stuck in the past, nursing grudges, accomplishes little in dealing with either the present or the future. Distinctness pushed too far produces separation—and the impossibility of full participation in a multicultural society.

Moving beyond the recognition of diversity to actually creating national unity in the new America will require reliance on some traditional Western values—openness, tolerance, equality—and what Thomas Jefferson in the Declaration of Independence referred to as "a decent respect." America is different from most other countries in the world because of its heritage as primarily a nation of immigrants. That fact is critical as we look around and assess the continuing influx of people from other places to the United States. Becoming rigidly set in particular ways or thinking in terms of a dominant group (or groups) have no place in a country whose demographic history reveals so many shifts in patterns and such variety. Moreover, in crafting a national self-definition meaningful for our times, it is important to acknowledge that prior efforts floundered as a result of excessive idealism or imprecise image construction.

"We live by symbols," Justice Oliver Wendell Holmes once remarked. For almost as long as the Republic, the symbol of America as a melting pot has occupied a dominant place in the nation's public mind. In 1782, six years after the drafting of the Declaration of Independence, a transplanted Frenchman J. Hector St. John de Crèvecoeur wrote of his adopted country in one of his inspired letters: "What then is the American, this new man? . . . Here individuals of all nations are melted into a new race of men, whose labours and posterity will one day cause great changes in the world." The image of a human melting process took root. In the nineteenth century, Emerson predicted "a new race" would be produced in "the smelting pot" America was becoming.

As immigrants arrived from the mid-1800s on, an ideal of a melting pot remained appealing. The almost mythic hold the symbol possessed was evident in 1908 and 1909 when a play called *The Melting Pot* became not only a Broadway hit but a national sensation. In that melodrama by Israel Zangwill about a Russian-Jewish immigrant, the protagonist declaims, "America is God's Crucible, the great Melting Pot" and "The real American has not yet arrived. He is only in the Crucible, I tell you—he will be the fusion of all the races, the coming superman."

Faith in immigrant assimilation leading to a shared quest for "life, liberty and the pursuit of happiness" was part of the romance of America. Second starts require hope. People willing to uproot themselves for new lives sought reassurance, and the symbol of the melting pot helped serve that purpose. As time passed, though, reality kept colliding with romance. Children of immigrants and their children found it difficult or impossible to achieve "the fusion of all the races." Ethnic, racial, and religious characteristics remained vital features for many Americans who did not want to sacrifice their heritage for the sake of one-culture-fits-all homogenization.

Recognition that some groups are "unmeltable" affirmed that pluralism and diversity are indigenous to the United States. New metaphors were coined. In recent years, there have been references to America as a "mosaic," a "tapestry," a "kaleidoscope," a "quilt," an "orchestra," a "weaving machine," a "tossed salad," a "mulligan stew," even a "stir fry." Vivid as these symbols might be, none has seized our imagination as did the melting pot. In fact, despite contemporary emphasis on the multicultural nature of America, the image of the fabled pot is so embedded in our thinking it continues to appear frequently. In *The Disuniting of America,* Schlesinger worries about fragmentation, asking "Will the center hold? Or will the melting pot yield to the Tower of Babel?"

Despite its enduring popularity, we should all come to an agreement that the melting pot symbol no longer holds water or anything else. America, even metaphorically, is neither an enclosed object (like a pot) nor a gastronomical delicacy (like a stew). It is a continuing and dynamic process, much closer in symbolic terms to a journey. Viewed collectively from this perspective, Americans are a heterogeneous people who go in one direction or another for a while, stop a spell, and from time to time get lost. It is a choice of roads taken or not taken, of detours and dead ends, of going together or going alone.

This idea of America as a journey is reflected repeatedly in our literature and popular arts. You see it in Mark Twain's *Adventures of Huckleberry Finn,* Walt Whitman's *Song of the Open Road,* Jack Kerouac's *On the Road,* William Least Heat Moon's *Blue Highways,* and Andrei Codrescu's *Road Scholar.* In movies, the theme is expressed in films as diverse as *Easy Rider, Lost in America,* and *Thelma and Louise.* Willie Nelson has made "On the Road Again" a contemporary anthem, and Bob Seger keeps riding "Against the Wind" in his popular song. On television, yesterday and today, there is *Route 66.*

However, to avoid getting overly sidetracked by discussing America as a journey, it is important to point out that the concept of assimilation generally—or ideally—connotes sacrificing one identity for another. While this phenomenon is possible for some people and their progeny, others either try and fail or (for any number of reasons) do not wish to make the attempt. Since the great immigration movements of the nineteenth century, there have been countless discussions of "hyphenated" Americans. Irish-Americans, German-Americans, Polish-Americans, Italian-Americans, to name a few, took their place in the United States, but retained a concern for their ethnic or religio-ethnic heritage. Today the designations have become broader—European-American, African-American, Asian-American, Hispanic-American—but the hyphen for many remains. As with the definition of multicultural, where—or whether—you put your emphasis becomes important. Accepting the first element before the hyphen recognizes diversity, but moving beyond the hyphen acknowledges a more encompassing identity, with obligations of citizenship and some sense of national unity. However, achieving the right balance of the hyphen has never been and will never be easy. Over a century ago, Herman Melville in *Redburn* wrote, "We are not a narrow tribe. . . . No: our blood is as the flood of the Amazon, made up of a thousand noble currents all pouring into one. We are not a nation, so much as a world. . . . "

With "a world" within one nation now more than before and assimilation an anachronistic objective in the eyes of a large number of people, what is the most appropriate and effective way for dealing with the dual concerns of diversity *and* unity? Michael Walzer suggests that the anything-but-simple hyphen can function "more like a plus sign" when ethnicity and nationality come together, noting further that "in the case of hyphenated Americans, it doesn't matter whether the first or the second name is dominant." But diversity by its nature implies separateness of one kind or another. The degree to which diversity is dominant surely does matter. Whatever exists to hold the disparate elements together should not be subordinate.

There is cruel irony in the fact that, at a time when traditional American values of democracy, egalitarianism, and free-market capitalism are finding greater acceptance around the world, the United States seems so unsure and tentative in coming to agreement about what common qualities or principles connect us as citizens of one country. The "metaphysic of promise" that Max Lerner celebrated in his classic work, *America as a Civiliza-*

tion, might retain its magnetic power for newly arrived immigrants, but the reality of contemporary conditions—urban decay, random violence, chaotic schools, conspicuous homelessness, plant closings, to name a few—temper the myth of an American dream for many others. Still, even amid such intractable problems and the continuing debate in scholarly precincts over the nation's decline, to avoid making the effort of finding and fostering the connections that unite all Americans is to make citizenship meaningless.

Since the country's first days, you find in many Americans a rewarding, indeed clarifying, case of dual vision. Simultaneously, they look to the past for the guidance that comes from basic, foundational ideals—freedom, equality, democracy, justice, self-determination—and they scan the horizon to discern how the future might see the realization of those ideals in their own lives. There was a recognition of being in the process of becoming. Most recently, there has been less of this dual vision for two notable reasons. The greater absorption in ethnicity and race has resulted in more focus on the particularized past, including a concern for victimization, and the optimistic hope of a boundless future has collided with blindingly real circumstances and problems.

How long this condition will exist—especially the decline of hope—is anyone's guess. However, for many it creates a barrier preventing full participation in a common enterprise for common good. Inspirational as he might have been as president, Ronald Reagan seemed uninterested in promoting programs to address domestic—and dividing—problems. George Bush shared the same policy indifference—while lacking the inspiring rhetoric. Indeed, according to the Republican analyst Kevin Phillips both Reagan and Bush engaged in "the politics of rich and poor," widening the distance between the haves and the have-nots. The growth at the extremes puts added pressure on the country's middle class, making the resolution of our problems even more difficult. Aristotle argued in his *Politics* centuries ago "that the best political community is formed by citizens of the middle class, and that those states are likely to be well-administered, in which the middle class is large, and stronger if possible than both the other classes, or at any rate than either singly; for the addition of the middle class turns the scale, and prevents either of the extremes from being dominant."

It is probably not coincidental that the controversy over multiculturalism crystallized during the Reagan and Bush years. Ideals, such as egalitarianism and self-determination, were continually being tested as the many learned about the few who were particularly successful. One can legitimately ask: Is it any wonder why some people seek the security from separation? If certain national ideals seem so remote as to be unreal, freedom permits the taking of other roads. However, the next question, of course, becomes: How far does a new road veer from the main one? The American journey can accommodate a number of parallel paths, but it is difficult to imagine routes leading anywhere that lose complete sight of the most heavily traveled way.

In *Democracy in America,* Alexis de Tocqueville rhapsodizes about millions of people "all marching together toward the same point on the horizon; their languages, religions, and mores are different, but they have one common aim." To be sure, there is always the fear that comes from a tyrannical majority, which values unquestioning conformity at the expense of diversity. However, the "one common aim" is the point to stress. What principles or beliefs today constitute the civil religion Tocqueville identified? Just where is this journey that is America taking us as the horizon of a new century approaches? It is becoming increasingly difficult to deal with, let alone answer such complicated questions.

Achieving the right balance for the diverse many in one multicultural society is the test now facing all Americans. To fail is to risk polarization, fragmentation, even tribalization. The violent extremes of ethnic, religious, and racial animosities now violate our sensibilities on a daily basis in Europe, Africa, and elsewhere. One only has to look at what has happened within what was formerly known as Yugoslavia to behold the newest definition of balkanization. The United States, of course, has endured its own bloody conflicts, including the rampage of killing, burning, and looting that followed the acquittal in the spring of 1992 of white Los Angeles police officers in the beating of a black man, Rodney King. The bedlam—variously called a riot, a disturbance, or a disorder—involved whites, African-Americans, Asian-Americans, and Hispanic-Americans. In the aftermath of the violence and in a trembling voice, King made an emotional statement that contained a question, "Can we all get along?" At once both strikingly simple and profoundly vexing, King's question might serve to concentrate the national mind on the opposing ideas of diversity and unity. Yet, as with other such concerns, this cannot be an argument over absolutes. The success or failure of functioning with the coexistence of diversity *and* unity will largely determine the future of America during the twenty-first century.

Postscript

"America and Multiculturalism" is the revised form of an academic paper first presented at the Fulbright Colloquium on "Citizenship and Rights in Multicultural Societies," sponsored by the Fulbright Commission at the University of Bologna in April 1993. The essay subsequently appeared in the Italian volume of proceedings *Cittadinanza e Diritti nelle Società Multiculturali* in 1994 and in an English edition from Keele University Press, *Citizenship and Rights in Multicultural Societies,* in 1995. Both books were edited by the conference directors Tiziano Bonazzi and Michael Dunne.

Reaction to the paper at the Bologna conference was, shall we say, mixed. Several of the Europeans understood the need for balancing national principles and multicultural concerns—without going too far in either direction. Some Americans, though, became animated in criticizing what they considered an overly nationalistic approach that failed to appreciate the merits of multiculturalism in education and elsewhere. When one fellow citizen announced, "You're no different from Rush Limbaugh," I realized that trying to chart a middle course about a subject with such strong proponents and equally strong opponents was probably hopeless.

Many people, alas, remain blind to the possibility of the dual vision I describe, a concept that is similar to but more positive than W. E. B. DuBois's notion of "double-consciousness." At the beginning of *The Souls of Black Folk*, DuBois wrote: "It is a peculiar sensation, this double-consciousness, this sense of always looking at one's self through the eyes of others, of measuring one's soul by the type of a world that looks on in amused contempt and pity. One ever feels his two-ness—an American, a Negro; two souls, two thoughts, two unreconciled strivings; two warring ideals in one dark body, whose dogged strength alone keeps it from being torn asunder." Tension between a particular background and the broader culture now affects millions more people than African-Americans; however, sensitivity to keeping the two dimensions in harmonious balance can lead to the dual vision that is proposed.

The term "multiculturalism" has become simultaneously loaded and threadbare in recent years. The single word evokes either a body of thought worth contemplating or the mind's back of the hand. What often gets lost in debates about multiculturalism is the need—yes, need—to re-think how Americans view ourselves and how we live together in a country that demographically is undergoing profound change. By 2050 immigration and birth-rate patterns will more than double the percentage of Hispanic-Americans and Asian-Americans living here.

Beginning in early 1998, the *Washington Post* devoted a considerable amount of space to a series, "The Myth of the Melting Pot: America's Racial and Ethnic Divides," with installments every month or so. The articles, filed from various regions of the country, probe what is happening today and the outlook for the future. Of particular concern is the notion of assimilation and how new Americans interact with and adapt to the existing culture and society. The melting pot is, indeed, a myth or romantic illusion, and assimilation means (among many other things) appropriating negative as well as positive characteristics. In this context, the media's questionable messages and consequences become important, particularly for younger immigrants learning how to behave and what to say. In a May 25, 1998 dispatch from Omaha for the *Post* series, William Branigin wrote:

> At work, not only in Omaha but in immigrant communities across the country, is a process often referred to as "segmented" assimilation, in which immigrants follow different paths to incorporation in U.S. society. These range from the classic American ideal of blending into the vast middle class, to a "downward assimilation" into an adversarial underclass, to a buffered integration into "immigrant enclaves." Sometimes, members of the same family end up taking sharply divergent paths, especially children and their parents.
> The ambivalence of assimilation can cut both ways. Many native-born Americans also seem to harbor mixed feelings about the process. As a nation, the United States increasingly promotes diversity, but there are underlying concerns that the more emphasis there is on the factors that set people apart, the more likely that society will end up divided.

Some divisions, of course, are inevitable. We are only human. However, divisions have a better chance of declining with greater concern for counterpoise between those people Arthur M. Schlesinger, Jr., refers to as "militant monoculturalists of the right" and "militant multiculturalists of the left." Balance is especially significant in education. What events and which figures will receive attention and emphasis in American history? Who will be read in studying our literature and why? How can students most effectively see the nation as a whole *and* the many, diverse parts that contribute so vitally to that whole? In *Americans No More,* Georgie Anne Geyer addresses these questions and related concerns with discriminating insight shaped by many years as a foreign correspondent.

Writing in *The New Yorker* in 1995, Andrew Delbanco quoted the letter of a young woman, an English major at "a distinguished liberal-arts college": "I have already read Langston

Hughes, Zora Neale Hurston, Amy Tan, Richard Wright, Malcolm X, Toni Morrison, Gabriel Garcia Márquez, Kate Chopin, Adrienne Rich, and Alice Walker. I have never had to read for school any Hemingway, Faulkner, Thoreau, Joyce, Steinbeck, James Fenimore Cooper, Blake, Melville, Jack London, Virginia Woolf, Milton, Poe, Donne, Keats, Shelley, Byron, Wordsworth, Wilder, Homer—the list goes on." Delbanco went on to note: "Her point was not that there is anything wrong with the inclusion of the first list but that there *is* something wrong with the exclusion of the second." As I argue in this book's last chapter, the either/or approach to many situations such as this one can be unduly limiting, if not, indeed, polarizing. Clearly, reading lists should reflect the range and breadth of our literature, the more recently canonized as well as the works of earlier influence. Instead of either/or, why not both/and?

One of the most trenchant appraisals of contemporary America comes from an outsider, an Australian, Robert Hughes, longtime art critic for *Time*. In *Culture of Complaint*, Hughes explains the different forces that contribute to "the fraying of America," the sense of an unraveling of the nation's fabric that so many people sense. Early on he argues:

> The fundamental temper of America tends towards an existential ideal which can probably never be reached, but can never be discarded: equal rights to variety, to construct your life as you see fit, to choose your traveling companions. This has always been a heterogeneous country and its cohesion, whatever cohesion it has, can only be based on mutual respect. There never was a core America in which everyone looked the same, spoke the same language, worshipped the same gods and believed the same things. Even before the Europeans arrived, American Indians were constantly at one another's throats. America is a construction of mind, not of race or inherited class or ancestral territory.

After dismissing the simplistic symbolism of a melting pot to describe what happens to people in the United States, Hughes observes: "Reading America is like scanning a mosaic. If you only look at the big picture, you do not see its parts—the distinct glass tiles, each a different color. If you concentrate only on the tiles, you cannot see the picture."

Yes. We all need to see "the big picture" *and* "the distinct glass tiles," the one and the many. However, the America of today and tomorrow is—and will be—the continuing journey that began yesterday and the many days before.

ALLIES OR ENEMIES?

The Uneasy Relationship between Blacks and Jews

By coincidence, the same week in February 1994 that *The New Yorker* published Paul Berman's essay "The Other and the Almost the Same," *Time* devoted its cover and thirteen pages inside to reportage about the Nation of Islam and to six perspectives of "The Rift between Blacks and Jews." A severe, almost menacing portrait of Louis Farrakhan dominated the cover, but the words delivered a sharper, more confrontational message. Under the heading "Ministry of Rage," *Time* said: "Louis Farrakhan spews racist venom at Jews and all of white America. Why do so many blacks say he speaks for them?" While Berman frames his argument for understanding the current relationship between African-Americans and American Jews with a sensitivity that sometimes seems strained, *Time* frightens readers by focusing on the conflict Farrakhan and his followers promote. The treatment by *Time* is typical of what we usually see in the mainstream American media, and an often overlooked factor in assessing how American blacks and Jews are actually getting along.

The Berman essay and the *Time* report—not to mention many other articles and broadcast segments—were provoked by a speech delivered on November 29, 1993, by Nation of Islam national spokesman Khalid Abdul Muhammad at Kean College in New Jersey. The speech received scant attention until January 16, 1994, when the Anti-Defamation League of B'nai B'rith published excerpts of it in a full-page ad in the *New York Times*

and other newspapers. That ad, with what became the widely
quoted claims that Jews are "the blood suckers of the black nation," that they "control" the White House and "own" the Federal Reserve, and that they are "most influential in newspaper, magazine, print media and electronic media," sparked the
firestorm throughout the communications world. Without the ad
and the subsequent coverage, Muhammad's vile ranting would
not have become a *cause célèbre*.

No one could rationally argue that the American public
should remain blissfully ignorant about the fomenting of hatred
and prejudice. However, in the current media environment, extremism in the cause of sensationalism is so common that forming an accurate picture of reality is increasingly difficult. Messages of conflict receive such amplification and magnification
they contribute to perceptions of hostility that are often more
profound, more "real," than what might be the actual circumstances of a situation. The research of George Gerbner and other
communications scholars proves that portrayals of violence serve
to make people more fearful of potential danger than the reality
of contemporary life warrants. Messages of conflict that dilate
on division deserve similar consideration. Of course, they reflect
phenomena worth appraisal; however, maintaining discriminating proportion and steady perspective is also crucial.

The paradoxical, even contradictory, extremes, presented so
sharply by the media, strain American culture. As noted in an
earlier essay, what we have today is a time of sensitivity *and*
shock. While some people go to extraordinary lengths to avoid
any slight or offense that could be construed in a negative light,
others seem inclined to go in the opposite direction for the sake
of being combative and confrontational. What is happening at
the margins of American life ends up in the mainstream media
because such occurrences conform to the contemporary definition of news (matters of change and conflict) and to the talk
show preoccupation of dealing with what is decidedly different or even abnormal. Incongruous as it might seem, a Madonna
or a Farrakhan are not that dissimilar in the eyes of the media.
These figures and others like them operate at the extremes, and

the emotions they elicit provide sensationalism that guarantees a response from a reader, listener, or viewer.

In Farrakhan's case, there is something ironic or mischievously humorous about his constant denunciation of the mainstream media. For instance, he said during an interview on Black Entertainment Television on February 19, 1994, that "the media in my judgment has a definite aim in the coverage, which is to inundate the people of America and the people of the world with their view of Louis Farrakhan, that he is a hater, a bigot, an anti-Semite, and the desire of this inundation of media coverage is to isolate Louis Farrakhan and make him a pariah, so that the next step which is the crucifixion or the destruction of Louis Farrakhan and the Nation of Islam could take place, and there would not be too much of a cry from the masses of the people." Complete with a crucifixion complex, he gains vitality and visibility when major communication sources direct their attention his way. Editors and producers know provocative speakers draw a crowd, so they willingly provide the modern soap-box.

For a demagogic *provocateur* like Farrakhan or his associate Muhammad, reality is largely rhetorical. Words even more than deeds give them a sense of strength and power. Satisfaction comes from greater amplification of their statements. More exposure means a wider potential audience. (*Time* devoted almost two full pages to the transcript of an interview with Farrakhan in its February 28, 1994 cover package, and he held forth for almost a full hour on *The Arsenio Hall Show* on February 25, 1994.) Although Farrakhan and other ministers of the Nation of Islam adopt stances that could be called intolerant and counter to this country's civil liberties, they effectively exploit certain rights to advance their cause—like the free exercise of religion, free speech, and freedom of the press. Censoring a Farrakhan is, of course, not an option; but censure or no coverage at all are two possible options for those in communications to choose.

Unfortunately, however, most anyone with a message that features conflict and controversy of an extremist stripe finds a place and gets a hearing in the current media culture of this country. The popularity of Rush Limbaugh, Howard Stern, Geraldo

Rivera, Jerry Springer, and other personalities who incite emotions attest to that. Advertising, too, reflects some of the characteristics we see in coverage and programming. Sharply negative political ads are so much with us nowadays because of the impact they have for forcefully capturing public attention and for lingering in a voter's mind. Farrakhan and others like him know the basic facts of modern media life and exploit them whenever possible. That is one significant reason why you see him and his Nation of Islam spokesmen talk at such length and intensity about American Jews. Like any blaze that involves fire trucks and the sense of an emergency, inflammatory language creates public interest. Today's media often turn a relatively small brush fire into a three-alarm conflagration.

Berman and other commentators on the relationship between African-Americans and American Jews focus on 1909 and the founding of the National Association for the Advancement of Colored People (NAACP) as the beginning of cooperation and common cause between the two groups. However, even before then and subsequently, you find an undercurrent of conflict, especially in the way blacks view Jews. In *The Souls of Black Folk* (1903), W. E. B. DuBois remarks, "Only a Jew could squeeze more blood from debt-cursed tenants." Richard Wright's autobiography *Black Boy* (1945) includes recollections a decade and more after 1909 that are representative as well as personal: "All of us black people who lived in the neighborhood hated Jews, not because they exploited us, but because we had been taught at home and in Sunday school that Jews were 'Christ killers.'" In the landmark study about Chicago, *Black Metropolis: A Study of Negro Life in a Northern City* (1945), St. Clair Drake and Horace R. Cayton state: "The inhabitants of the Black Ghetto grow restless in their frustration, penned in, isolated, overcrowded. During a depression or a war [the periods covered by this account], the consciousness of their exclusion and subordination is tremendously heightened. Within this spatial and social framework morale tends to be low and tempers taut. Anti-Semitic sentiments are latent. Demands for the economic and political control of the Black Belt arise." Later, there is discussion of "an or-

ganized anti-Semitic drive" that took place in 1938 against Jewish merchants, the group blacks dealt with most consistently and
extensively for so many years.

Despite all that has been written about the black-Jewish alliance during much of the twentieth century, one wonders how
much was well-meaning rhetoric of civic-minded elites and how
much genuine, broad-based cooperation among the people in
general. Organizational leaders and activists of one kind or another received considerable attention for working together, most
prominently throughout the Civil Rights movement of the late
1950s and early 1960s. However, on a day-to-day, person-to-
person basis among non-elites, tensions still conditioned attitudes. In retrospect, what happened during the late 1960s proves
critically influential to the relationship between African-Americans and American Jews. For a number of reasons, the undercurrent of conflict surfaced and then affected elites and non-elites
alike.

The rise of the Black Power movement, beginning in 1966
(not long after the killing of Malcolm X in 1965), helped foster
a mentality of separatism and group identity in contrast to the
drive for integration that had animated so much of the earlier effort for civil rights. As James Baldwin wrote in response to some
efforts of black nationalists then: "Negroes are anti-Semitic because they're anti-white." Moreover, the 1967 Six-Day War in
the Mideast focused the attention of American Jews on Israel
as an endangered Jewish homeland, enhancing group identity
among Jews here and abroad.

The next year, 1968, brought President Lyndon Johnson's
withdrawal for re-election because of the Vietnam War, the assassination of Robert Kennedy, the anarchy of the Democratic National Convention in Chicago, and the November election of
Richard Nixon and Spiro Agnew as president and vice president,
and these events were profoundly important to the course of
American political life. The year 1968 was also pivotal in the relationship between African-Americans and American Jews. The
assassination of Martin Luther King removed the most charis-
matic and eloquent integrationist from the Civil Rights move-

ment, opening the way for Black Power advocates to have much greater say in racial politics and other matters. That same spring, the report of the Commission on Civil Disorders (often called the Kerner Commission) said that two Americas existed, one white and one black, and that a massive governmental effort was needed to (as the report concluded) "shape a future compatible with the historic ideals of American society."

In September 1968, Rabbi Meier Kahane, an extremist not terribly different in approach from what Farrakhan would subsequently become as he embraced the opposite view, formed the Jewish Defense League in Brooklyn by, in part, playing off fears of the rise in black anti-Semitism and black-on-Jew street crime. The teacher strike in New York that same fall pitted African-Americans against American Jews in a protracted conflict that not only intensified emotions but sharpened divisions between the two groups. *Time* magazine (in its January 31, 1969 issue) had as its cover story "Black vs. Jew: A Tragic Confrontation," with the New York strike the prime subject for treatment. The picture of an African-American carrying a sign appeared on the first page of the story. The hand-lettered sign read: "Jews get out of Palistine [sic]. It's not your home anyway! Moses was the first traitor and Hitler was the Messiah!!!" The references to Palestine (meaning the territory occupied by Israel during the Six-Day War) and to Hitler drove home the heightened animosity and focused on one group's poisoned view of another.

As individual groups in America—like the blacks and the Jews—became more absorbed in concerns affecting them, there was less attention paid to a common agenda of intergroup cooperation. Rather than looking ahead to that most-American of hopes, "a better tomorrow," African-Americans and American Jews turned inward and looked backward. Blacks traced their feeling of victimization, oppression, and anger to the brutality of their forced departure from Africa and the institution of slavery in this country before the Civil War and the Emancipation Proclamation. Jews angrily remembered the brutality and mistreatment that bloodied their history, especially the rampant anti-Semitism in Europe during the past century. What many commentators called "the radical evil" of the Holocaust concentrated the Jewish mind and made the defense of Israel's existence a paramount concern. When United Nations Ambassador Andrew Young met with representatives of the Palestine Liberation Organization, Jews interpreted this action by an African-American as a direct threat to the survival of Israel and pressure grew for his departure, which occurred in 1979. Once again, there was open, heavily reported conflict between blacks and Jews, something that would be repeated in 1984, when then-presidential candidate Jesse Jackson referred to New York as "Hymietown."

Farrakhan's defense of Jackson marked the first time the Nation of Islam leader spoke out in public and at a high volume against Jews. That is when he called Judaism "a gutter religion," Israel "an outlaw state," and Hitler "a very great man." For over a decade, Farrakhan has been at the center of the increasingly knotty relations between African-Americans and American Jews. His oratorical skill and penchant for going to extremes to shock creates huge audiences; however, his message has so many different aspects to it that it is difficult to focus on one or two points. Contradictions abound. He is a religious figure who openly espouses hatred and prejudice. He is the supporter of black nationalism and separatism who actively seeks government contracts and support. He is a radical militant who preaches a lifestyle and dress-code that could be classified as strictly conservative. In addition, he says he is an advocate of truth, but he builds many of his arguments on lies.

Making sense of these contradictory elements is a challenge often leading to confusion, which can result in his followers, enemies, journalists, and others being selective in what they focus on and emphasize. A case could be made, in fact, that many African-American listeners to his multiple-hour orations find more meaning and value in his message about personal responsibility than in his denunciation of whites in general and Jews in particular. In short, what matters most is variable, depending on the viewpoint of the recipient for a particular message. To a certain extent, this accounts for his standing in segments of the black community and, by contrast, the intensity of animosity directed at him by so many others.

To be sure, however, much of Farrakhan's appeal and news-worthiness comes from his fiery rhetoric and its verbal scare tactics. Taylor Branch, the author of *Parting the Waters* and *Pillar of Fire*, a multi-volume history of "America in the King Years," observed in a May 1989 *Esquire* article that "any black man who can make white America leap on its chair in fright or revulsion will win the generous admiration of suffering black America for the sheer guts of the deed." Farrakhan's speeches blame white America collectively for the plight of black America, and it is curious that since 1984 he has singled out American Jews for some of his angriest outbursts. For heaven's sake, many wonder, why does he do it? In part, it is because of the historic undercurrent of anti-Semitism within the African-American community. In part, it is because the specificity of attacking a particular group allows him to direct his fire and identify a distinct scapegoat. And, finally, in part, it is because of post-Holocaust sensitivity to anti-Semitism. Farrakhan is shrewd and knows statements running counter to this sensitivity will receive the wide amplification he craves.

There is also something wickedly clever in his and the Nation of Islam's emphasis on Jewish involvement in the American slave trade. No one with elementary awareness of historical facts puts any credence in the book *The Secret Relationship between Blacks and Jews,* yet Farrakhan constantly promotes this bogus and misleading work to link Jews directly to the defining experience of oppression and victimization for African-Americans. He preys on present-day fears and problems by evoking a past that never happened. When he also says that "the black holocaust was a hundred times worse than the holocaust of the Jews" and that Hitler possessed attributes of greatness, he twists the most central facts and symbols of anti-Semitism to his purposes, enraging many in the process. You see a definite pattern, a deliberate strategy of provocation, to his statements since 1984, the time when he has gained national notoriety. Sadly, while Farrakhan has become a household name and received extensive coverage, problems within the African-American community (especially urban areas) have gotten more serious, if not critical. Attention to him, however, often obscures or overshadows journalistic efforts to portray these problems in ways that might ultimately lead to action. William Raspberry, a black *Washington Post* columnist who is widely syndicated, won the 1994 Pulitzer Prize for commentary for eloquently addressing social conditions and concerns. However reasoned, his we're-all-in-this-together views are, unfortunately, less well-known than Farrakhan's among Americans, regardless of their race, ethnicity, or religion.

This said, it is legitimate to inquire how representative Farrakhan might be in talking about the relations between African-Americans and American Jews. To what extent should he be taken seriously as a commentator on this subject or any other? Does his ability to gain media visibility translate into genuine impact among blacks? Or are we dealing with someone who gets attention for being outrageous but has relatively little effect, especially in the way African-Americans view American Jews? The February 28, 1994 issue of *Time,* with its cover story about Farrakhan, includes telling public opinion results of a survey involving African-Americans. Here are the findings for three of the questions:

Do you think Farrakhan's opinions and behavior improve relations between blacks and whites in this country?

Improves	12%
Makes worse	31%
Has no effect	34%

Do these groups have too much power?

	Yes
Whites	80%
Big corporations	69%
Jews	28%
Catholics	26%
Labor unions	21%
Blacks	2%

Have relations between blacks and Jews gotten better or worse?

Better	26%
Worse	16%
Haven't changed	42%

Moreover, in an extensive survey of intergroup relations by Louis Harris for the National Conference of Christians and Jews, which was released March 2, 1994, African-American views of Jews were, in the main, more anti-Jewish—but not to an alarming degree when viewed in the context of other responses. The question "When it comes to choosing between people and money, Jews will choose money" brought agreement from 54 percent of African-Americans, 43 percent of Latino-Americans, 35 percent of Asian-Americans, and 27 percent of non-Jewish whites. For the question that Jews have "too much control over business and the media," 43 percent of African-Americans agreed, compared to 37 percent of Latino-Americans, 35 percent of Asian-Americans, and 22 percent of non-Jewish whites. When asked whether Jews are "too preoccupied with their history of persecution, such as the Holocaust," 49 percent of Latino-Americans responded affirmatively—as compared to 45 percent of African-Americans, 44 percent of Asian-Americans, and 31 percent of non-Jewish whites.

What is revealing about these numbers is the relative consistency of opinion among the three minority groups: African-Americans, Latino-Americans, and Asian-Americans. Even more compelling are the findings about integration. Sixty-six percent of whites support "full integration," with 71 percent of African-Americans, 72 percent of Latino-Americans, and 85 percent of Asian-Americans favoring the same objective. Given Farrakhan's tremendous emphasis on the Jews being to blame for many ills among African-Americans and his support of separatism, even a return to Africa, survey research does not reflect extraordinary influence in these areas. Why, then, in recent opinion surveys of African-Americans does he personally rate so highly—second to Jesse Jackson in the ranking of black leadership and a favorability rating of two-thirds of those polled? We are forced to go back to what Farrakhan says about self-reliance, self-respect, and self-discipline and its resonance in the black community rather than his indictments of the Jews and his calls for his particular kind of nationalism. With the disturbing levels of unemployment, child poverty, drug addiction, crime victimization, and teen pregnancy among African-Americans, a figure preaching about a lifestyle of self-control leading to personal success is bound to receive a hearing from people hoping or praying these problems can be overcome. One might even inquire: What could be more American?

In Studs Terkel's oral history, *Race: How Blacks and Whites Think and Feel about the American Obsession,* Clarence Page, a syndicated columnist for the *Chicago Tribune,* directly addresses and confronts Farrakhan's media appeal as opposed to his actual impact:

> Black-Jewish tensions have been considerably overblown by the media. The coverage of Louis Farrakhan says it all. Among the great many black people, he's rated as useful and entertaining. An educated clown. People will fill Madison Square Garden and watch him for his entertainment value. How many have joined his movement? Very few. He can say anything and the media will rush out there.
>
> When I worked for Channel 2 [in Chicago], they chartered a plane and flew me and a crew to Indianapolis to cover a routine Farrakhan speech. We had to put it on the air that night. It was his usual stuff, nothing extraordinary. I know why they sent me down there. They were hoping he'd say something outrageous. This is their thing.
>
> Naturally, Farrakhan welcomes all this attention. What respect he has from black people comes to anybody who stands up to white folks and tells it like it is. My wife was thrilled when I took her to see him. She heard so much about him as entertaining. Did she become a follower? No. There is a side of us as black people that resents the way we are ignored as individuals, the way mainstream America insults us. In a way, Farrakhan is feeding off that sentiment. (p. 362)

Page is not alone among African-Americans in seeing the media as largely responsible for exacerbating tensions between blacks and Jews. The militantly iconoclastic writer and University of California at Berkeley professor Ishmael Reed is much more critical of the mainstream press. In his collection of articles, *Airing Dirty Laundry,* Reed notes: "The underlying irony of the highly publicized and exaggerated black-Jewish feud is that Jewish Americans and black Americans face far more problems from members of 'white' ethnic groups than from each other. Neither group has as much power to destroy each other as their enemies have to destroy them both." A few paragraphs later in his essay "Is There a Black-Jewish Feud?" he draws on his own experience to sharpen his point that media sound and fury signify a reality he does not know:

> Most of the African American intellectuals who are trotted out by the media to comment about racial issues are unknown in the black community and don't even reside there. As someone who lives in what journalists refer to, lazily, as an "underclass" neighborhood—which means that my neighborhood includes blacks who are high class, middle class, and lower class, some with a lot of class and others with no class—I can testify that I have never heard any of my neighbors make an anti-Semitic remark; nor have my black neighbors burned a cross in the yard of those homes or apartments in which the few whites on this block reside. When we have our neighborhood crime watch meetings, people from all backgrounds show up. (p. 39)

Reed's personal report might not reflect the way things are in, say, Crown Heights, New York. But, as he points out, "Crown Heights is not your typical black community," what with the presence of the Lubavitcher sect of Hasidic Judaism and a large number of West Indian people of color. Incidents, such as what happened in Crown Heights in 1991 and 1992, are portrayed in the media as black-Jewish hostility, which is true but only to a point. Specific circumstances demanding historical and social context get lost in coverage that seeks to be symbolic or symptomatic when, in fact, it is actually singular.

Back in 1922 in the book *Public Opinion,* Walter Lippmann warned of the dangers of stereotypes clouding or creating a barrier for more complete understanding of complex reality. Both blacks and Jews have already had to deal with unflattering and unfair representations in American popular culture for much of this century. The carefree, shiftless black and the scheming, money-hungry Jew were stock figures out of central casting, promoting negative images that still exist today. It is the responsibility of those in contemporary journalism to keep reports about conflict, especially what might be perceived as intergroup conflict, in perspective and to avoid treatment that overly simplifies or stereotypes. Unfortunately, in a cluttered media environment the expression "what bleeds leads" captures the thinking of many in communications who are fighting among themselves for attention and the audiences that attention brings. Restraint and sober judgment frequently get short shrift in a frenzy of competition.

Paul Berman's faith in a return to "emancipatory liberalism" offers some hope for the future, despite the continuation of the pattern of conduct described by French philosopher Vladimir Jankélévitch that identifies how people "almost the same" interact with one another: "Love, hatred; a wobbling back and forth from one to the other." What is worrisome, however, and not explored by Berman, is the prevalence and potential influence of Farrakhan and like-minded individuals within American education. Khalid Abdul Muhammad's speech that caused so much debate took place on a college campus, a favorite place at the current moment to spread his notions. Leonard Jeffries of City College of New York and Tony Martin of Wellesley College espouse views in academic settings about Jews that most non-Jewish observers would classify as anti-Semitic. The use of *The Secret Relationship between Blacks and Jews* as a textbook in classes around the country also gives one pause about what the young might be learning. Fabricating "history" is a far cry from revising it, but few students have the knowledge to make discerning judgments about distant "facts" being presented to them. Combine what is taking place in sectors of academe with some of the media coverage that accentuates conflict between African-Americans and American Jews and many young people would find talk of historic alliances and being "almost the same" as irrelevant to what they have been taught and learned. Minds thusly shaped suggest a rosiness to the future that is more thorny than blooming. If, however, educators and intellectuals take a stand to expose the errant extremism currently in fashion in several quarters, then the future might resemble the past, complete with both fraternity and hostility.

Berman's imaginative adoption of Jankélévitch's theory provides a useful, if somewhat forced, analytical frame with which to study the relationship between African-Americans and American Jews. As Berman explains the theory that helps structure his argument:

> Since emotional relations fall under the star of irrationality, people who are almost the same might flip-flop into loving one another, bedazzled by their wonderful point of commonality. Or they might sink into confusion about the intensity of their feelings. "When you are in a state of passion, you don't know if you love or if you hate, like spouses who can neither live together nor live apart," Jankélévitch said.

In *Broken Alliance: The Turbulent Times between Blacks and Jews in America* (1988), Jonathan Kaufman offers another approach, a more metaphorical one, for understanding this particular intergroup interaction. Kaufman observes: "The alliance between blacks and Jews was not a natural one. It resembled an Indonesian gamelan symphony, in which each instrument plays its own tune, following its own score. For most of the time, the music sounds dissonant. Then, at certain moments, the music wells up as all the instruments blend together in harmonious symphony. But the instruments continue playing their separate scores. The dissonance can return."

. The dissonance, if you will, has become more pronounced in recent decades as Jews have achieved a more central place in American life. Historically outsiders, they now occupy key insider positions in large numbers throughout all realms of the professions, government, commerce, education, and communications. This collective success story in no way undercuts their traditional allegiance to anyone perceived as oppressed or suffering prejudice. However, sharper, more readily noticeable differences exist between American Jews and African-Americans today than earlier in the century.

Near the end of "The Other and the Almost the Same,"

Berman notes, "It was the past that made the blacks and the Jews almost the same, and the past has the singular inconvenience of never going away." The past, in history and memory, demands our constant attention. As Justice Oliver Wendell Holmes once remarked, "Continuity with the past is not a duty; it is only a necessity." But the future, too, deserves continuing consideration and an avoidance of extremes. Attempting to shape that future in harmony with animating principles of the common good is another necessity—especially as American ideals of equality and promise struggle to become reality for restless and searching people from many different backgrounds and beliefs.

Postscript

Paul Berman's essay, "The Other and the Almost the Same," helped initiate a new conversation about the historic ties and contemporary disagreements between African-Americans and American Jews. The journal *Society* reprinted Berman's article and used it as the springboard for nine other assessments of "Jews, Blacks, and Others." My contribution, originally titled "Past Accord and Present Dissonance," appeared in the September/October 1994 issue of *Society*. Berman subsequently brought together nineteen essays in his edited anthology, *Blacks and Jews: Alliances and Arguments,* also published in 1994.

In leading the Million Man March in Washington, D.C., on October 16, 1995, Louis Farrakhan remained in the spotlight and attempted to broaden his appeal. Commentators on the March and Farrakhan, including several African-Americans, criticized the exclusion of women in the event and the absence of a coherent, inclusive program for political and social action once the marchers disbanded and returned home.

Farrakhan, however, continues to be an example of a new kind of Darwinism in our contemporary media: survival of the most outrageous and sensational. Deciding whom to feature and what to emphasize is a daily—and, in some cases now, hourly—choice confronting journalists responsible for a program or publication. With so many sources competing for attention, the loudest, most extreme voices get heard, with passion or vitriol often crowding out reason. Farrakhan, of course, knows this media environment very well, and he is shrewd in gaining press access and in guarding against overexposure.

Despite his strategic use of the media and some public, post-1994 overtures to get along more amicably with American Jews, Farrakhan bears watching for the influence he has within the Nation of Islam and the wider African-American community. The intensity of his personality—as magnified and amplified by the media—can skew the public's perception of what is actually happening at a given time and also reduce any possibility of creating common purpose among people, regardless of their religion, race, or other characteristics. Although serious illness in the late 1990s reduced his personal appearances and interaction with the press, Farrakhan represents a distinct line of thinking and action of potential consequence—and conflict—in the future.

RUNNING SCARED

"This is America," said the father whose small son, with a crushed skull and several other injuries, fought for life in the Oklahoma City hospital. "We shouldn't have to run scared. We shouldn't be afraid to take a two- or three-year-old to the day care center."

Spoken in the somber aftermath of the Alfred P. Murrah Federal Building bombing on April 19, 1995, as an act of anti-government extremism, the words resonate beyond that single evil deed and capture a larger national mood. In recent years, running scared and being afraid have increasingly become typical responses to life in the United States.

Trying to come to terms with contemporary America means wrestling with a conundrum. Throughout the twentieth century, peace and prosperity have been the principal and enduring objectives of the nation. Yet today, with the U.S. unchallenged as the only superpower in the post–Cold War world and the economy by most statistical measurements relatively strong, fear and worry seem to haunt Americans as never before. Doubts crystallize into questions about who we are as a people and where we might be going in the future.

One way of approaching our time is to see it as an Age of Insecurity. So many traditional patterns have been broken of late that we nervously wonder what lurks around the corner—at work, in the home, and down the street. A traditionally forward-looking people now keep glancing over their shoulders.

The most striking fact about our insecurity is its virulence. No aspect of life is immune, and no person unaffected. Not long after the Oklahoma City bombing and a succession of maddening assaults, the White House closed off Pennsylvania Avenue to all vehicles, symbolically becoming much less open—but far more secure.

Fear of crime and violence lies at the heart of personal insecurity. By the year 2000, it is estimated we will be spending over $100 billion annually on private security measures, five times the amount paid in 1980. Since 1960, the American population has grown by 43 percent, but the number of violent crimes (murder, rapes, assaults) has increased by more than 550 percent.

According to government estimates, 83 percent of Americans will be victims of violent crime at least once, and over half of all homicides are now committed by strangers. The random nature of these acts, exemplified by the phenomena of "drive-by shootings" and mail-bomb explosions, contributes to a generalized sense of danger, especially in our cities.

Tragically, young people between the ages of twelve and fifteen run the greatest risks of being victims of violence, according to a 1995 Justice Department study. In Chicago, to take one example, sixty-seven children were murdered in 1994, three more than the previous year, when the *Chicago Tribune* devoted space on page one to every killing of a person under the age of fifteen. Finding guns in schools is depressingly commonplace nowadays in small towns and metropolises alike, with the young not immune from using them against teachers and fellow students.

Besides this personal insecurity, there is a growing sense of social insecurity that comes in large part from the changing nature of the family structure in America and the great influx of immigrants, legal and illegal, into the country. The most recent Census Bureau statistics show that half the children in the U.S. live outside the traditional nuclear family of a married couple residing with their biological offspring.

Divorce and out-of-wedlock births are, of course, factors, with the rate of illegitimacy particularly alarming. In 1960, 5 percent of births occurred outside of marriage. By the end of the century, it is estimated that the number could jump to 40 percent. Today 70 percent of prison and reform-school inmates come from fatherless homes, and that level is expected to rise dramatically. Senator and scholar Daniel Patrick Moynihan has noted that we are "defining deviancy down" at a time of "volcanic change in family structure, for which there is no comparable experience in human history." One analyst of social trends calls what is happening "excessive individualism," unbridled self-indulgence that never considers the long-term consequences of actions.

Demographically, too, America is undergoing profound change, which is unsettling to many. Approximately 11 million immigrants arrived during the 1980s, the most ever, with people of Hispanic and Asian heritage leading the way. In 1950, 89.5 percent of the population was classified as "white." By the turn of the century, the percentage will be right around 70. The Census Bureau statistics report that one of every ten Americans was born abroad, with sizable communities gathering in certain cities and regions. The controversies surrounding multiculturalism and diversity that have roiled the nation in recent years revolve, in part, around these demographic shifts, which challenge the traditional patterns of the country's make-up. Anything new can be off-putting, and this is particularly true with human difference.

What you might call cultural insecurity is another dimension to the larger condition of our age. Schools and popular communications are principal carriers of culture, and we can all point to examples of excellence in education and throughout the media. Yet, with stunning frequency, horror stories about what is happening in schools set heads shaking. Are drugs and alcohol that prevalent? Can students be planning their own funerals instead of their future lives? Is academic achievement possible in such conspicuously deteriorating buildings and settings so lacking in basic educational needs?

It does not take an expert in media analysis to see that several segments of the communications industry seem hell-bent on seeking a level of audience engagement well below the lowest human common denominator. Messages of all kinds effortlessly arrive in our homes on printed pages, television channels, videotapes, radios, CDs, tapes, and computer screens, and many of them do little more than contribute to the defining of our culture downward. Unfortunately, they are so much with us it is next to impossible to avoid them. Not without reason, the loudest applause President Bill Clinton received during his 1995 State of the Union speech came when he denounced "the incessant, repetitive mindless violence and irresponsible conduct that permeates our media all the time." Other political figures, notably former Vice President Dan Quayle and former Senator Bob Dole, have made similar statements to much public approval.

Notwithstanding cheers supporting criticism of the media in general and Hollywood in particular, political insecurity pervades America. Since 1990, citizen anger and cynicism have fueled our politics, with the desire for change a dominant concern. The results of the 1992 presidential and 1994 mid-term elections were resounding votes to shift direction, to have new people grapple with persistent problems. The electorate's discontent is so strong that we see volatility rather than stability. Democrats benefited in 1992, and the Republicans in 1994.

To make matters worse for those in public life, confidence in our national government has fallen dramatically during the past three decades. In 1964, according to the Gallup Organization, 75 percent of the people trusted Washington "to do what is right all or most of the time." In 1994, the number had sunk to 19 percent. Credibility is essential in a democracy, and the duplicity, if not downright lying, that took place in the Vietnam War, Watergate, and the Iran-contra affair profoundly affected the nation's psyche. Widespread disillusionment resulted, leading to (among other things) the growth of militantly antigovernment groups across the country—and, ultimately, to the tragedy in Oklahoma City.

Of even more central concern to millions of Americans than discontent with politics and government is the nagging, day-in and day-out sense of economic insecurity—for now, the near future, or some later time. Ever since 1973, the median family income has remained static in real terms, a marked contrast to the period between 1947 and 1973 when median family income consistently rose and, in fact, doubled. For the past several years, real family income has actually declined for the majority of Americans. "Downsizing" and "corporate restructuring" have become common business practices in recent years, producing not only greater profits but nervous worrying about employment possibilities, health care coverage, and pension benefits.

More than in any other Western country, the gulf between rich and poor is widening in the United States. However, the lives and expectations of people in the middle class have undergone the most pronounced change. The rise in technology in all phases of work and the decline in high-wage manufacturing jobs (along with the shifting of jobs overseas by international companies) have helped create what's now called "an anxious class." Interestingly, though, there are currently more unemployed white-collar workers than blue-collar ones. Gone are the days of career-long devotion to one employer, with a gold watch and happy retirement the reward of a worker's continued service.

The economic insecurity so many now feel is all the more troubling because it runs directly counter to traditional ways of thinking about the country and its promise of opportunity. The much-fabled "American dream"—with secure employment and upward mobility leading to the purchase of a home and even greater prosperity for the children of that household—now seems less achievable, more remote, even romantic.

To be sure, the different types of insecurity—personal, social, cultural, political, and economic—exist at varying levels of intensity among us, but they also converge and intertwine to yield a general attitude about the state of the country. Anyone listening to America today hears a persistent grumbling and griping.

People are anxious about tomorrow because it seems so different from yesterday. Problems fester without being resolved. The simple rhythms of life snag themselves on unforeseen complications. There is a feeling of betrayal from the past, with its national spirit of optimism, and a persistent sense of powerless-

ness. Troubled times with their internal turmoil breed everything from fear about safety at a shopping mall to paranoia that
malevolent forces abound, just waiting to attack.

Curiously, though, when you begin to look more deeply at
survey research measuring public opinion, you see a striking difference between how people assess what is happening in the
country and how they view their own situations. Between the fall
of 1991 and the spring of 1995, the Gallup Organization on
twenty-six occasions asked the question: "In general, are you
satisfied or dissatisfied with the way things are going in the
United States at this time?" At no time did the number of those
"satisfied" go above 39 percent and the average was 28.6 percent. The "dissatisfied" reached 84 percent once and averaged
68.3 percent.

But a *Times Mirror* survey conducted in 1994 attempted to
measure "satisfaction with how things are going in country,
community and personal life." Twenty-four percent said they
were satisfied with the nation's course, corroborating the Gallup
polls and others charting whether the country is going in the
right or wrong direction. Interestingly, 68 percent expressed
community satisfaction, and 83 percent personal satisfaction.

What creates such divergence between the national and the
personal? In part, it is possible that some of our sense of insecurity is propelled or magnified by the media, with their absorption
in the abnormal and aberrational. Conflict and controversy—
rather than contentment—draw audiences, and a steady diet of
vividly portrayed stories clearly has a cumulative impact on how
we perceive the country. Paradoxically, the effects are simultaneously sensitizing in making us aware and desensitizing in making us think we as individuals can do very much to deal with our
national problems.

In addition, journalists by nature are attracted to change as
moths to light, and we keep being startled by the new. Fads and
outrages quickly come and go, but the media dutifully report
them. The fixed spotlight on change makes people curious—but
jumpy. Is all this happening now? What about me? How will I
cope with the future?

Clearly, however, it is not fair to deposit all, or even most, of the blame on the media. The realities of our times are primarily responsible, with a common element being all of the consequential change that surrounds and bombards us. We repeatedly hear phrases with the word new in them: the new global economy, the new communications, the new morality, the new demographics. It is as though the ground we regularly walk keeps moving under us on a daily basis. Security that comes from stability, knowing life's grooves, is less possible. What might have been learned or believed in an earlier time, like the Baby Boom period after the Second World War, no longer seems to apply.

Besides trying to cope with the pattern-breaking present, Americans are, to a certain extent, experiencing the consequences and aftershocks of the three previous decades with their turbulence. The 1960s, in particular, unleashed forces of such power and influence that they continue to have meaning to the culture and society.

The civil rights revolution at first and later the women's movement sought to open doors previously closed because of a person's race or gender. The goal of equal access to education, employment, housing, voting, and other aspects of American life animated both causes, profoundly changing the country. The rise of the counterculture and explosion in new media with out-of-the-mainstream sources of entertainment occurred simultaneously, challenging traditional ways of thinking and acting. What happened was more than a youthful fling of rebellion or a short-term "generation gap." The wide-ranging efforts of political and governmental reform, which took place following the upheaval of the 1968 Democratic Convention in Chicago and the Watergate scandal, transformed our politics and created a vastly different electoral process.

None but the least reflective, unrepentant reactionary could fail to see the value of much that was achieved in the 1960s. With dizzying regularity, we saw sincere efforts to address problems, to expand opportunity, to open up a closed social system, and to enhance democratic participation. In very real ways, many of the actions of this period helped America to become closer in practice to the nation we have always celebrated in the ideals of the Founders' statements and the authors of civics books.

Unfortunately, however, in more recent years what began in the 1960s with worthwhile intentions has changed markedly and produced results that contribute to our Age of Insecurity. It is as though some people involved in whatever movement or cause carried matters too far, well beyond the original goals and into territory with consequences that often contradict earlier objectives. To be specific but by no means inclusive:

- Instead of working to achieve integration, we now hear calls in cities and on college campuses for separation and group allegiance. Nation of Islam leader Louis Farrakhan and like-minded speakers pack auditoriums across the country to rail against the white majority and specific segments of it, while African-American, Hispanic, and Asian-American students demand dormitories of their own at certain schools.
- Instead of the counterculture's desire for an Age of Aquarius, it now seems Anything Goes, especially in the different forms of popular culture that caters to younger Americans. Watching MTV for a few minutes or listening to some examples of "gangsta" rap shows how different the 1990s are from the 1960s in this regard. "Just Do It" is more than a shoe company's slogan, and the suggestion of irresponsibility in those three words speaks volumes about our time.
- Instead of opening smoke-filled rooms and providing greater citizen access, we now have a chaotic nominating system for presidential candidates that the cartoonist Rube Goldberg might have designed in his most-inspired moment of imaginative lunacy. The bonds between campaigning and governing have never been weaker in this country, and the new system that requires millions of dollars of special interest money makes many a worthy White House aspirant decide against even getting involved. A flawed process is bound to yield flawed products. Recent history not only confirms this but contributes to an overall decline in political confidence.

Interestingly, some of what we see happening around us today follows patterns similar to ones of earlier eras and sketched out in this book's first chapter. With any study of this country's history, you come to recognize that wretched excess occurs quite naturally in America and exists as the underside of freedom, of going too far for whatever reasons. As noted earlier, all you have to do is consider how the West was really won or how the work of the temperance movement ultimately led to the establishment of Prohibition. More recently, besides the already-noted examples, you have had merchants of obscenity and other vileness hiding behind the virtues of the First Amendment and, in certain circumstances, proponents of affirmative action making a case for what more closely resembles reverse discrimination.

In other words, the impulse to excess grows naturally in the American soil, and it is far from being a new phenomenon. But this nation's health or well-being requires the constant search for broader consensus about the common good and avoidance of extremes as much as possible. In our case, it is a matter of working to find the right balance between liberty and authority, between individualism and community, between freedom and equality, between rights and responsibilities, between economic prosperity and social justice, and between demographic variety and national unity.

Achieving a greater sense of equilibrium—and security—will be anything but easy because of the tangled web of personal, social, cultural, political, and economic factors that crisscross and influence each other. However, many of the problems feeding this insecurity have moral dimensions that all of us can recognize and do something about. One social thinker has remarked that "the great wave of moral deregulation began in the mid-1960s." This "moral deregulation" is the darkest legacy of the 1960s, and its cost is the moral deficit we are now experiencing. Until individuals and institutions begin in a concerted way to devote themselves to doing what they can to deal with this deficit, it is difficult to imagine that we will see much—or, indeed, any—of this kind of change.

However, the prime question that our Age of Insecurity provokes is: Are we seeing the first stages of America's decline as a country and civilization? Publication of Paul Kennedy's *The Rise and Fall of the Great Powers* in 1987 triggered a continuing debate between "declinists" and "revivalists"—those who think conditions in the U.S. reveal inner decay beyond repair and others who believe the nation can right itself by returning to the basic principles that shaped American life for over two hundred years.

It is possible, of course, that the "declinists" are right, that our slide won't stop and we will go the way of other once-dominant civilizations, whether it be Rome of ancient times or the British Empire of the nineteenth century. However, given the relative recency of many of our problems, this line of thinking seems terribly premature—and out of character with what previously happened when the country faced other crises, even in this century, such as the Depression and the Second World War.

In the wake of the Oklahoma City bombing, several commentators drew defining-moment comparisons between that violent act of infamy and the attack on Pearl Harbor in 1941, which propelled America as a nation into a fight for survival in World War II. Bringing an end to our Age of Insecurity will take a similar collective, comprehensive effort as the country mounted at that time.

Then, however, there were definite, easily identifiable enemies engaged in declared war. It was a black-and-white situation. Today the adversaries are internal, and they change depending on one's perspective. Some people, for instance, might accuse politicians or the government, others the media, still others specific groups or population segments—such as the rich, the poor, the new immigrants, or the extremists with allegiance to a cause. Instead of being a black-and-white matter, it is a murky, depressing gray, with Americans against Americans in what often seems uncivil conflict.

And how do our domestic discontents and circumstances strike outside observers? Writing in the British newspaper the *Guardian* (June 10, 1995), Martin Woollacott remarked: "Europeans, bombarded with the O. J. Simpson trial, killings after chat shows [on television], the Waco siege, the lyrics of Nine Inch Nails, or the Oklahoma bombing, are beginning to see America, not as a powerful society with serious problems and some bizarre corners and bad moments—it has always been that—but as a deranged and dangerous place."

Whether the United States continues to be perceived as "a deranged and dangerous place" will test each of us, and what we do to try to correct the reality of this perception will largely determine America's future.

Postscript

"Running Scared" was first published in the autumn 1995 *Notre Dame Magazine*. The Oklahoma City bombing was a stunning blow to the American body politic, leaving the nation alarmed at an act of extremism that seemed both coldly calculating and humanly incomprehensible. How much further can hatred of the government go? What does such a horrific act more broadly signify? Why? Why? Why?

Since the blast and its aftermath, the mood of the country has changed. More people seem satisfied with what is happening and America's current direction. In large measure, of course, these public opinion surveys reflect the continuing strength of the economy, the balancing of the federal budget, the bullish stock market, and the low level of unemployment. We not only vote our pocketbooks on Election Day, as the old saw says, but we respond to pollsters in a similar way. At the same time the economic statistics are up—and help make Americans more upbeat—rates of crime and out-of-wedlock births are down.

Despite these favorable signs, the relative contentment of the late 1990s coexists with social and cultural conditions that raise serious questions about the future. According to the report "A Nation of Spectators" of the National Commission on Civic Renewal, which was released in mid-1998, the United States is the industrialized world's leader in wealth, power, and influence—*and* murder, violent crime, imprisonment, divorce, abortion, sexually transmitted diseases, teen suicide, cocaine consumption, and pornography. As troubling as these facts might be, the conclusion about what we are doing—or not doing—to deal with our problems is equally depressing. The report states: "Never have we had so many opportunities for participation, yet rarely have we felt so powerless. In a time that cries out for civic action, we are in danger of becoming a nation of spectators."

Feeling powerless and being disengaged are not characteristics of a healthy and secure society. The sunny mood polls now reflect mask a deeper discontent, if not disillusionment about the moral direction of the country. Listening to the discussions of the possible motivations for the series of school shootings perpetrated by teenagers in the spring of 1998, and even more shockingly the tragic carnage at Columbine High School in Littleton, Colorado, in the spring of 1999, brought to light underlying fears about the future and what it might hold.

Nicolaus Mills traces the sources and offers context for this *angst* in his book *The Triumph of Meanness: America's War against Its Better Self.* Quoting from books, articles, film scripts, song lyrics, even bumper stickers and t-shirts, Mills documents that the meanness engulfing the 1990s has become "a state of mind, the product of a culture of spite and cruelty that has had an enormous impact on us." Whether it be negative political advertising, dehumanizing rap music, gory video games, or the bareknuckle barbarism of what is called "ultimate fighting," Americans are constantly dealing with the opposite of what Abraham Lincoln referred to (in his memorble phrase) as "the better angels of our nature."

Running scared is one response to these times. But running away from the excesses of meanness, spite, cruelty, and worse solves nothing—and a disaffected or alienated nation of spectators over time becomes incapable of doing what is required to make the necessary changes.

COPING WITH HYPERDEMOCRACY
AND HYPERCOMMUNICATIONS

For better or worse, television invariably transforms whatever it transmits. Marshall McLuhan and his disciples notwithstanding, the medium is *not* the message. But the medium of communication does, indeed, affect how a message is presented and how it is received. In the case of television and American political life, the medium has profoundly changed the way public figures go about their work and the way the public perceives politics and government.

Lyndon Johnson dilated on this subject with characteristic color after he retreated from the White House and returned to private life on his ranch in Texas. As David Halberstam tells it in *The Powers That Be,* during a break in the interviewing for Johnson's televised memoirs, a CBS producer asked the former president "what had changed in politics between his early days in Congress some thirty years before and the final days of his presidency. [John] Sharnik asked his question quite casually and was stunned by the vehemence of Johnson's answer. 'You guys,' he had said without even reflecting. 'All you guys in the media. All of politics has changed because of you. You've broken all the machines and the ties between us in Congress and the city machines. You've given us a new kind of people.' A certain disdain passed over his face. . . . 'They're your creations, your puppets. No machine could ever create a Teddy Kennedy. Only you guys. They're all yours. Your product.'"

Johnson had learned his style of politics in the old school of retail, one-on-one relationships. He had also served as vice president under John Kennedy, a president who recognized the power of the image and the importance of using television as the newest "bully pulpit." That pulpit, of course, has grown in significance and variety since the 1960s, and we do, without question, have "a new kind of people" in politics. The presidency itself is a different institution because of television. A constant in recent years is that change in communications will occur, and that change will affect what happens in political life.

Ronald Reagan's approach to governing that dominated the 1980s is already passé. Having "a line of the day" operating within a more comprehensive and choreographed strategic plan is less possible today because of growing media fragmentation and new definitions of news. For example, the evening newscasts of ABC, CBS, and NBC no longer possess the for-the-record, almost ritualistic, significance they once did in the life of the country. A citizen today can no longer automatically expect a report about the president or the administration on any day's agenda of stories. Indeed, in recent years, as the antipolitical mood of the citizenry has grown, there has been less coverage of Washington on the nightly news programs and greater emphasis on medical and consumer stories.

Be that as it may, television is still the modern pulpit for a president. Understanding the significance of that pulpit and what is called the "rhetorical presidency" in its contemporary manifestation requires, at least in part, knowledge of the various forms of communication delivering presidential rhetoric—or what passes these days for presidential rhetoric. Looking closely at Bill Clinton can be fruitful because he is aware not only of the new world of communications—where (among other occurrences) "narrowcasting" has replaced "broadcasting"—but the continuing importance of more traditional ways of presenting words or ideas to the nation and the world. Moreover, his experience is a case study in the limitations of the "rhetorical presidency" in trying to bring about governmental change.

The presidential campaign of 1992 was unlike any other in American history. In addition to the speechifying to which we have become accustomed in the twentieth century, the 1992 race also featured more access to the candidates during talk-show formats of one kind or another. Television and radio air-waves hummed with political discourse (or, in some cases, chatter), creating more openness and greater emphasis on longer explanations of problems and their possible solutions. Unlike, say, 1988, which featured the ten-second sound-bite and the thirty-second negative spot, 1992 offered extended presentations that drew audiences and created a sense of greater public involvement. The debates that year proved more popular than any pundit predicted, and the three presidential candidates (Bill Clinton, George Bush, and Ross Perot) appeared ninety-six times on just five television talk shows (*CBS This Morning, Donahue, Good Morning America, Today,* and *Larry King Live.*)

Articulate, indeed garrulous, Bill Clinton was a beneficiary of this new political-media environment. Regardless of the situation, words tumbled out of his mouth with such ease it was reminiscent of certain Southern speakers of the nineteenth century celebrated for the tall tales they could spin. Although 1992 ended up being primarily a referendum on George Bush and whether he should continue as president, Clinton's ability as a communicator (in traditional and nontraditional situations) helped his cause, engendering hope and optimism about what he might do in office.

Unfortunately for him, however, the public mood shifted quickly. Future historians of the Clinton presidency will assess his first several months in office by using such phrases as "an awkward beginning," "a stumbling start," or "an error-prone opening." In addition to mishandling key appointments, making gays in the military an early (and controversial) priority, waffling in foreign affairs, and receiving a much-discussed $200 haircut, the president had an unsophisticated, some might say immature, approach to communication in these early days. He waited sixty-three days after his inauguration before conducting his first press conference (on March 23, 1993). Five days earlier, he had told those assembled at the dinner of the Radio and Television

Correspondents, "You know why I can stiff you on the press conferences? Because Larry King liberated me by giving me to the American people directly."

Intelligent as Clinton clearly is, he was slow in seeing the importance of sustaining a strategy of communication that augments and advances his policy initiatives and actions. The rhetorical aspect of the public presidency—what we hear and see as citizens—did not receive the focus or emphasis it deserves. The president found it difficult to pass by a microphone without saying something. Unfortunately, when anyone talks incessantly on many subjects, it becomes difficult for a listener to recognize what is most significant and meaningful. Subsequently, the listener often pays less attention to the speaker.

Clinton, however, broke himself of this habit late in his first term, and then did what he could to avoid saying anything after charges of political and sexual scandals began to swirl in 1997. By shifting from one extreme to another, it is difficult to see the realization within the White House that effective governance today is very much a balancing act—between statecraft and stagecraft, talk and action, traditional forms of communication and newer ones, campaigning and governing, domestic concerns and international affairs, and principle and pragmatism. It is less a matter of making either/or decisions. Rather, a continuing both/and situation creates the perception, if not reality, of equilibrium and stability.

What happened with the Clinton health care reform proposal is illustrative of the out-of-balance, unmethodical presidency that created early doubts about the nation's chief executive. Despite a pledge to have legislation ready within a hundred days of taking office, Clinton did not send the 1,342-page "Health Security Act" to Congress until October 27, 1993, six months past the announced date. A month before, the president had delivered a nationally televised address to Congress on September 22, 1993, and this passionate call to action was met with not only applause but general public approval. Then, however, several weeks and events intervened (including the killing of twelve

American soldiers in Somalia on October 3). Momentum was lost, the rhetorical opportunity squandered. Other voices, coming from both sides of the aisle in Congress and a barrage of television ads from special interest groups, competed with the president's—and eventually prevailed in the debate.

As we saw with the health care reform initiative, Bill Clinton can be a commanding and compelling speaker. Who can forget his 1994 State of the Union Address with its dramatic gesture of waving a pen that he threatened to use in vetoing legislation that did not provide "every American private health insurance"? But the oratory often does not translate into action because there is either delay or a lack of deliberate, purposeful follow-through. In this circumstance, rhetoric lacks its intended effect, making no lasting contribution.

After the Republicans assumed majority control of the House of Representatives and the Senate with the mid-term elections of 1994, Clinton approached the situation of divided government warily. Yet in an oddly ironic way, the new condition ended up helping him politically. He could play to his strong suit of campaigning and delivering moving speeches—without any great expectations by the public of his getting significant new policy initiatives passed. Subsequently, he himself announced the era of big government to be over. Dramatizing small steps (for example, advocating school uniforms, teen curfews, or the v-chip for new televisions) became his style of governing. With the economy strong and no dangerous foreign entanglements, the president won re-election in 1996 and remained popular, despite the onslaught of negative, scandal-related coverage.

To a certain extent, Clinton is a pivotal president. Deft usage of new types of political communication helped him come to power, and on several occasions he has shown mastery of traditional forms, whether in speeches to Congress or in his press conferences. He is also quite aware of the new political-media environment that is currently emerging. In an interview with Brian Lamb of C-SPAN on February 17, 1995, Clinton discussed the phenomenon of "hyperdemocracy" that the web of modern, instantaneous communications creates. Acknowledging that the technology can make possible "a stampede based on the emotion of the moment," he went on to note: "But Andrew Jackson once said that the cure for any problem of democracy was more democracy. . . . So what I think we need to do is not recoil from the democracy, the hyperdemocracy, but try to work through the more irrational and destructive aspects of it to have a national conversation again." Having "a national conversation again" is one thing, and well worth fostering. But is it possible to stop at the talking stage without moving to action—say, voting from home not only for candidates but policy proposals of one kind or another?

Later in the interview, the president turned his attention to what he termed the "hyperinformation" now available to "the average American voter every day." He admitted that "there is an enormous obligation on the president . . . to get a message through there [that] requires enormous discipline and focus and concentration. . . . But I didn't organize and deploy the resource properly to make sure that we had communicated what we had done and how it fit into the vision that I ran for president to pursue."

The concepts of "hyperdemocracy" and "hyperinformation" deserve more explicit attention in coming to terms with both the present and the future. Dictionary definitions of the prefix 'hyper' ("over, above, or in great amount" and "in abnormal excess") should hoist warning flags in the minds of people. However, an America with "hyperdemocracy," "hyperinformation," or "hypercommunications" is by no means a distressing prospect for certain influential citizens. The proliferation of sophisticated communications technologies has also led in recent years to a chorus of calls proposing that the people use interactive capabilities of these technologies to participate in decision-making about governmental issues. During his 1992 presidential campaign and more recently, Ross Perot has talked—to the enthusiastic approval of listeners—about the value of "electronic town-hall meetings" with people providing feedback on public issues and questions. In his book *Arrogant Capital,* Kevin Phillips praises the new methods of political action made possible by modern communications. Phillips writes: "Futurists Alvin Toffler and John Naisbitt emphasize two reasons for rightly calling our system of representative government outdated: First, what used to be true representative government is being swallowed up by the Washington presence of more interest groups than the world has ever before seen in one place. Representative government has become interest-group government. Second, new electronic technology now gives governments an unprecedented wherewithal to empower the ordinary voter directly. We should use it." If we are to believe such thinking, electronic plebiscites loom over the horizon, providing a continuous flow of opinions or judgments to elected and appointed governmental officials.

In theory, the idea of direct democracy in some form appeals to a primordial characteristic of American citizenship. Getting together in town meetings to discuss and resolve problems goes back to the early years of the nation. In addition, there is the romance that anyone, with or without experience, can recognize what is in the best interests of the people and act accordingly. An innocent, well-meaning amateur—like Jefferson Smith in Frank Capra's film *Mr. Smith Goes to Washington*—rapidly learns how to confront antidemocratic activity and work on behalf of the citizenry. An attitude of "anybody can do it" is common among Americans. Especially at a time of widespread public mistrust, the sense of control that comes from a greater say in political life is alluring.

However, the theory and romance of direct democracy quickly collide with the realities of public ignorance about details of governance and relatively low rates of voting in existing electoral procedures. At jeopardy in any plan to conduct regular referenda with the people deciding is the basic character of our representative system. It is hopelessly idealistic (and misguided) to imagine that the average citizen as a matter of daily routine will study complex legislation and initiatives to prepare to vote on an ongoing basis. As David Mathews explains in *Politics for*

People, almost half of the bills that come before the U.S. Congress include highly technical and specialized scientific data.

Cheerleading from the likes of Ross Perot, Kevin Phillips, Alvin Toffler, or John Naisbitt notwithstanding, that technology makes direct democracy possible does not mean that we should create such a process. The dawning of a new century provokes an abundance of futuristic speculation; however, sober-minded remembering of the nation's first two centuries reveals the enduring value that comes from a system stressing balanced and deliberative governance. While the modern media work with wondrous speed, people in political life need to guard against making decisions when public opinion is highly volatile and still shifting amid the transmission of new information.

We already see the makings of a "cybermob" in the pressure exerted on politicians via letters, phone calls, faxes, and e-mail when talk-show hosts decide to get listeners or viewers to speak out on a particular issue. In certain respects, it is difficult to tell the difference between an old style interest group and a new, technologically mobilized faction. To be sure, only a contemporary Luddite would reject out-of-hand any use of the new information technologies in our politics and government. Throughout his valuable book *The Electronic Republic,* Lawrence Grossman argues that we need to re-invigorate our commitment to citizenship at the same time we consider what role these technologies might play. He concludes his discourse with this reasoned statement:

> As we go about the complicated task of reshaping representative government and redistributing political power in the electronic republic, we must retain the delicate constitutional balance between local and national, between private interests and the public good, and between minority freedom and majority rule. Those will not be easy tasks. But we cannot afford to miss the opportunity to use these new means of communication for the public benefit. We must harness the interactive telecommunications system to help make modern deliberative democracy satisfy the needs of far more citizens than it does today. (p. 254)

American political life, most notably the presidency, and the world of popular communications have been intertwined since the days of pamphleteering and the partisan press. The separate realms influence and have impact on each other—with the public placed in a role akin to "observer-participants" or "consumer-citizens." In *The Road Ahead,* computer guru and entrepreneur Bill Gates remarks:

> Each media advance has had a substantial effect on how people and governments interact. The printing press and, later, mass-circulation newspapers changed the nature of political debate. Radio and then television allowed government leaders to talk directly and intimately with the populace. Similarly, the information highway will have its own influence on politics. For the first time politicians will be able to see immediate representative surveys of public opinions. Voters will be able to cast their ballots from home or their wallet PCs with less risk of miscounts or fraud. The implications for government may be as great as they are for industry. (p. 271)

But the question becomes: How far should we go? Can democratic action be carried to an extreme or to an excess that ultimately becomes self-defeating or dangerous? Is hyperdemocracy healthy for the body politic? After discussing how "the highway will bestow power on groups of citizens who want to organize to promote causes or candidates," Gates considers the possibility of carrying that power to its furthest point, what he calls "total 'direct democracy'":

> Personally, I don't think direct voting would be a good way to run a government. There is a place in governance for representatives—middlemen—to add value. They are the ones whose job it is to take the time to understand all the nuances of complicated issues. Politics involves compromise, which is nearly impossible without a relatively small number of representatives making decisions on behalf of the people who elected them. The art of management—whether of a society or a company—revolves around making informed choices about the allocation of resources. It's the job of a full-time policymaker to develop

expertise. This enables the best of them to come up with and embrace nonobvious solutions direct democracy might not allow, because voters might not understand the trade-offs necessary for long-term success. (p. 272)

Astutely and appropriately, Gates draws the line at using the burgeoning technologies in ways that fundamentally and irrevocably alter the traditional relationship between the citizen and government. No one disputes the value of using whatever the communications media offer as a way to be better informed and more participatory. Such work is, indeed, commendable—and should be strengthened through education programs and by efforts supported within the communications industry. If the media over time can help cultivate a more knowledgeable, engaged electorate, democracy itself would be a beneficiary. Possibly—just possibly—there would be less public discontent and more reason to become civically involved.

Before the promise of a purer, more direct form of democracy inflames too many minds, a contemporary case-study of unintended consequences shows the weaknesses, if not evils, of a particular type of hyperdemocracy. The lunacy of the current nominating system for presidential candidates makes one pause and wonder whether enhancing participation is an unalloyed benefit to the welfare of the Republic. Indeed, what has happened in the past three decades gives credence to Samuel Coleridge's shrewd observation that "[e]very reform, however, necessary, will by weak minds be carried to an excess, that itself will need reforming." In *America in Search of Itself: The Making of the President 1956–1980*, Theodore H. White remarked: "There was a terminal madness to the primaries of 1980—the madness of a good idea run wild." After explaining that the post-1960s system is "a classic example of the triumph of goodwill over common sense," the noted chronicler of presidential campaigns wrote: "There was no longer any way of making a simple generalization about how Americans chose their candidates for the presidency. What was worse, no school, no textbook, no course of instruction, could tell young Americans, who would soon be voting, how their system worked. And if we of the political press had to cram such rules into our heads as we moved from state to state, each with two parties, and each state differing—how could ordinary voters understand what professional observers had such difficulty grasping?"

White's book appeared in 1982. The system, alas, has become even more maddeningly complicated since then, with states for varying reasons continuing to jockey for more advantageous positions. Though originally intended to foster democratic openness and citizen participation, the current design defies simple explanation by the media or anyone else, and voter turnout is generally quite low. Residents of states later in the process feel as though they have little or no voice in a process that rewards the people able to participate earlier.

Clearly, the reforms need reforming to make the process more fair and representative—possibly randomly scheduled regional primaries spread out over a few months. The various instruments of political communication can render a service in this regard. Greater awareness of the myriad weaknesses of the ever-changing procedure could ultimately yield concern throughout the citizenry that election to our national offices (president and vice president) demands a methodically designed and implemented nationwide nominating system. Until reform occurs, however, the media—complete with their institutional characteristics and biases—will continue to be responsible for "nationalizing" the contests that take place in the individual states, idiosyncratic as they tend to be.

It could be argued that heavy coverage of a chaotic process contributes to the chaos, making matters and how they are perceived even worse. Journalists, though, could point out the genuine problems of this type of hyperdemocracy, particularly the change, contingency, and personality-orientation the current procedure tends to promote for the nation as a whole. In *Breaking the News*, James Fallows writes:

> The ultimate reason people buy the *New York Times* rather than *People,* or watch *World News Tonight* rather than *Entertainment*

Tonight, is a belief that it is worth paying attention to public affairs. If people thought there was no point even in hearing about public affairs—because the politicians were all crooks, because the outcome was always rigged, because ordinary people stood no chance, because everyone in power was looking out for himself—then newspapers and broadcast news operations might as well close up shop too, because there would be no market for what they were selling. If people have no interest in politics or public life, they have no reason to follow the news. It doesn't concern them. (pp. 243–244)

Although somewhat limiting in defining news, particularly in a multisource environment, Fallows's statement suggests that information with a political or public dimension should mean something in the lives of the people. Simultaneously consumers of media messages and citizens, people need to see the relevancy of the news for themselves—such as the case in nominating presidential candidates. Otherwise there is the danger that people will assume the role of spectators and (in times of scandal) voyeurs, watching the passing scene without recognizing any personal or civic connection to it. Should it happen, the marriage of hyperdemocracy and hypercommunications will lead to a public that—in popular parlance—is "hyper" about politics in general.

In preparing for the future, it is important to realize that the changing communications environment will place new and different demands on the citizenry. The proliferation of media outlets means constant competition for a person's attention and the finite amount of available time one can spend with the media's messages. With so much information and entertainment from which to choose, people will have to be more active in seeking out news about politics and public affairs. Unless they already understand the significance of their involvement in civic life, they might be inclined to seek any of the multitude of diversions the same media offer in abundance.

Interestingly, with CNN, C-SPAN, web sites on the Internet, and many other sources, the average citizen has a virtually unlimited opportunity for access to data about every aspect of

American democracy. Worries about coping with the information overload notwithstanding, the most compelling concern centers on the following question: Will individuals—except for the self-interested engaged in politics and government—take the initiative to study issues and ideas relevant to democratic deliberation? In recent years, as the number of television channels has grown and the use of the remote control operator has become more popular, the phenomenon of "zapping" messages without immediate appeal has increased. Somehow or other, the slow-moving and complicated processes of public life will have to be perceived as worthy of continuing consideration, or the public knowledge central to purposeful action will suffer even greater decline.

The implications of "hyperdemocracy," "hyperinformation," or "hypercommunications" on the presidency and American political life in general are, to say the least, profound. Questions abound: How can someone govern and lead at a time when so many different messages (political and nonpolitical) are coming from so many different sources? What is the most effective way to deliver messages when there is so much fragmentation in communications? What can a president expect the people to know at any given time? How responsive should a president be to passions of the moment that might be whipped up by opponents using the new media technology?

These are not questions that can be easily answered. What is clear, however, is the challenge that now exists to the traditional American patterns of political thought and action. As Grossman suggested earlier, there now exists, as never before, a threat to the Founders' vision of not only representative but deliberative democracy, complete with different branches of government and their so-called checks and balances. Momentary passions would cool over time, the thinking went, and the Republic would not lurch one direction one day and another way shortly thereafter. Countervailing political forces could achieve some sense of consensus or equilibrium, but it would not happen overnight.

In this new world, which promises even more possibilities of instantaneous communication in the future, a president will have to learn to deal with what Clinton already termed "the blizzard of stuff" swirling in the media and also discover ways of cutting through all of the communications clutter to deliver messages that have resonance and meaning within the larger context of an administration's goals. If this means appearing on MTV to communicate with a constituency that is usually not tuned-in to other, more traditional sources of information, so be it. In short, a president will need to go where the people are and make the administration's case with creativity and authority. But a knotty follow-up question that emerges from this new condition is: How is it possible to be accessible to different kinds of media (both old and new) *and* also retain what you might term "presidential stature" that, in part, comes from maintaining the proper distance and aura? As before, it will be a delicate balancing act, requiring shrewd judgment and concerted effort.

A president, however, is not the only figure who will have to change in adapting, bravely or otherwise, to this new world. With the much-ballyhooed "information superhighway" just around the corner, having access to 500 television channels that converge technologically with several on-line computer services will require citizens to be considerably more resolute in seeking information about politics and government. Troubling as it might sound, the wealth of communication outlets could ultimately result in a poverty of political knowledge. The Jeffersonian dream of citizens sharing a common body of facts or ideas in deciding what is best for the nation will be more difficult to achieve because so many other sources of information will compete for the public's attention. In this new political-communications environment, will we be willing to accept these new obligations of citizenship? Will whoever is president be successful enough—in rhetorical terms—to lead us to this new relationship between the elected and those doing the electing? Will we be able to guard against going too far to avoid the threats of hyperdemocracy and hypercommunications?

Near the end of his life, James Madison wrote in a letter to a friend, "A people who mean to be their own governors must arm themselves with the power which knowledge gives." Modern media make the potential for that kind of power much more accessible than Madison, or Thomas Jefferson, or any of the other Founders ever imagined. For the vitality of American democracy now and in the future, citizens must actively assume the responsibilities such knowledge and power make obligatory for effective, purposeful self-governance. To do otherwise would not only endanger our political system but place at risk our distinct—and distinctive—civilization.

Postscript

After writing a book, *Demanding Democracy,* about the 1992 presidential campaign and the new, uncharted involvement of the different forms of media in American political life, I was asked to participate in the Brigance Forum on "Leadership, Rhetoric, and the American Presidency" at Wabash College and to contribute a paper for the deliberations of the U.S. Department of Education's "Democracy at Risk" project, coordinated by Harvard University's Kennedy School of Government, the University of Maryland's Center for Political Leadership and Participation, and Washington State University's Edward R. Murrow School of Communication.

What I wrote for the Brigance Forum publication, which appeared in 1996, and for the book *The Public Voice in a Democracy at Risk,* edited by Michael Salvador and Patricia M. Sias and published by Praeger in 1998, amplified some central points first made in *Demanding Democracy.* "Coping with Hyperdemocracy and Hypercommunications" brings together these concerns and other related material into a single essay within the context of this volume's theme. The intention is that what appears here will serve as a cautionary statement about American politics and communications—and going to extremes in troubling ways.

BEING PRESIDENT WHEN ANYTHING GOES

Never at a loss for plain-spoken yet provocative statements, Harry Truman once told a White House gathering, "The president of the United States is two people. He's the president and he's a human being."

Making a distinction between the nation's highest office and its temporary occupant helps explain the complex way Americans view and remember presidents. Despite what's been called "the glorious burden"—with its powers and responsibilities, pomp and circumstance—the human element is never too far from public consideration for anyone reaching the pinnacle of our political system.

Even George Washington—he who was "first in war, first in peace, and first in the hearts of his countrymen"—endured civic complaint when he traveled by carriage rather than horseback for a brief time. The king of England rode in a coach; the president of the new United States did not. Washington returned to his horse—albeit with a gold-trimmed saddle cinched over a leopard skin that citizens judged appropriate for the man and his office.

From the early days of the Republic until today, presidents have engaged in a delicate balancing act. For the sake of popular support, they have sought to be perceived as having common bonds with the electorate at large. At the same time, though, they have wanted that same electorate to see them as elevated enough in stature to be worthy of the trust to govern a nation with many dreams and its share of nightmares.

108

This continuing, democratic interplay between being "one of us" and "above the others" assumes special importance in assessing personal aspects of a public figure. That Andrew Jackson grew up in humble, log cabin surroundings and became a much-celebrated military hero proved influential in seeking the White House during the 1820s. And his nickname of Old Hickory established rapport between this new kind of American leader—the previous six presidents had been aristocratic but not monarchical—and people he hoped would follow. Both his up-from-the-bootstraps biography and his distance-reducing sobriquet established traditions subsequent presidents adapted for their purposes.

In fact, William Henry Harrison in 1840 defeated Jackson's vice president and one-term successor, Martin Van Buren, by being portrayed as a hard cider-loving commoner with a log cabin upbringing. Harrison, actually the son of a wealthy Virginia planter, and his fellow Whigs felt compelled to use Jackson's techniques, complete with their human appeal, to be competitive. Bending the truth was just one trick in a campaign that strictly followed the manager's edict: "Let him [Harrison] say not one single word about his principles, or his creed—let him say nothing—promise nothing. . . . Let the use of pen and ink be wholly forbidden as if he were a mad poet in Bedlam."

Early in our history, the preoccupation with image and image-making rooted itself in the American political soil. Party-sponsored newspapers provided information with a definite partisan viewpoint, with much of the news either championing or castigating public figures of the time. Matters personal as well as ideological became popular journalistic subjects.

Even then the private lives of presidents played a role in press coverage. James Callender, a former supporter of Thomas Jefferson, turned on the man from Monticello, publishing a story in 1802 that the president was involved in an affair with one of his slaves. "By this wench Sally," Callender wrote, "our president has had several children. There is not an individual in the neighbourhood of Charlottesville who does not believe the story, and not a few who know it." Thus was born the long-disputed story of a relationship between Jefferson and Sally Hemings.

Genetic testing nearly two hundred years after the allegation first circulated offered evidence that the most cerebral of the Founding Fathers probably had fathered at least one of Hemings' children. This disclosure provoked a flood of commentary about the author of the Declaration of Independence as a hypocritical slave master, who deplored miscegenation in his writing, a neglectful parent, and, in the eyes of some, a possible rapist. Yet, even with the new information, profound questions persist. "We know more than anybody," notes Daniel P. Jordan, president of the Thomas Jefferson Memorial Foundation, "and we don't know anything about the nature of that relationship."

All the recent coverage and the previous historical debate underscore the compelling human curiosity surrounding the presidency. As civics books point out, whoever occupies the office is chief of state, chief executive of the federal government, commander-in-chief of the military, principal diplomat, and leader of a political party. While these interwoven roles define official responsibilities, personal traits and characteristics often determine how Americans respond to a president.

Whether it be "Honest Abe" Lincoln's absolute sincerity to preserve the Union, Theodore Roosevelt's rambunctious loquacity, Franklin D. Roosevelt's sunny self-confidence in dark times, Harry Truman's snappy candor to go with his common touch, Dwight Eisenhower's serenely reassuring avuncularity, John Kennedy's self-effacing magnetism, or Ronald Reagan's eagle-soaring optimism and humor, these human factors helped establish and maintain connections with the public of intangible yet substantial consequence. Complicated governmental policies or choreographed political maneuvers merge with personal attributes in the citizenry's assessment.

By its nature human response of this kind is subjective—a feeling with emotional ties that contributes to an overall opinion. Since Washington's time but with more dramatic emphasis during the twentieth century, the various forms of communications have served as principal couriers in forming the impressions Americans carry around in their heads about public figures.

Gone are the days of a partisan press more committed to shaping stories for electoral advantage than to an accurate portrayal of our political life. Now, robustly independent and competitive media provide words and pictures that place sustained, at times ceaseless, attention on the White House. First with film and later with videotape and live-shot television technology, presidents present themselves with concern for stagecraft as much as statecraft. How we perceive the personality being projected is particularly important, given the institutional decline of political parties and the rise of independent-minded ticket-splitters.

Looking at the broad sweep of presidential history, we see that the way journalists defined news at different times has greatly influenced what the public knew about their highest elected leaders. For instance, private matters received attention in the nineteenth century with the published rumors about Jefferson and the intrusive coverage of Grover Cleveland's honeymoon in 1886. (When Cleveland, a 49-year-old bachelor, married 22-year-old Frances Folsom, they never expected reporters to spy on their activities during a six-day wedding sojourn in Maryland. But newspaper readers learned in detail what the couple ate, wore, and did.)

Even before reaching the White House, Jackson and Cleveland had to contend with personal stories intended to kill them politically. During the 1828 campaign, Andrew and Rachel Jackson were pilloried in opposition newspapers for engaging in adultery, because they had married several decades earlier without knowing that Rachel's divorce from her first husband had never become official. Jackson's victory that year was tempered by the fatal heart attack his troubled wife suffered before the inauguration. Despite a legendary iron will, Old Hickory would never be the same.

In 1884, Cleveland, a Democrat, overcame press charges that he had fathered an illegitimate child years before he became active in politics. Although the Republicans' battle cry—"Ma! Ma! Where's my Pa? Going to the White House. Ha! Ha! Ha!"—became popular, when it was reported that Cleveland accepted financial responsibility for the child and didn't deny the possibility of paternity—the actual fact was in doubt—the matter died down. Later, Cleveland's supporters shot back their own response to the competition's taunting question: "Gone to the White House. Ha! Ha! Ha!"

Although it seems difficult to imagine, for much of the twentieth century journalists—and hence the public—avoided extensive discussion of the private lives of presidents. When the United States assumed a more prominent role on the world stage after the Spanish-American War and World War I, presidential power grew. With it came more deliberate control of information about the president by public relations-minded associates.

For instance, mystery and secrecy surrounded Woodrow Wilson's last seventeen months in the White House after he suffered two strokes in 1919. It wasn't until the publication of Gene Smith's *When the Cheering Stopped* in 1964 that the whole story of First Lady Edith Wilson's presidential pinch-hitting became general knowledge. Working with a doctor, she shielded Wilson from government officials and the public, carrying out official business in his name.

People working for Wilson's successor, Warren G. Harding, resorted to blackmail and government suppression of a book to help hide Harding's protean philandering. Four years after his death in office in 1923, one impecunious mistress, Nan Britton, wrote *The President's Daughter* about their affair, assignations in an Oval Office closet, and their illegitimate child. Since the late 1920s and especially in recent times, behind-the-scenes memoirs about every aspect of White House life have become dubious yet suggestive sources that help to balance and complement orchestrated presidential image-making.

Understanding a president often requires making connections between the public figure's pre-White House years and subsequent days in office. As Robert Shogan points out in *The Double-Edged Sword*, Theodore Roosevelt's sickly childhood and youthful insecurity stand in marked contrast to his leading the Rough Riders and to his strenuous (yet "bully") life in politics. TR's early struggles, in Shogan's words, "generated a relentless impulse to demonstrate his strength and forcefulness by imposing his will on others and, along with that, making himself the cynosure of all eyes. 'Father always wanted to be the bride at every wedding and the corpse at every funeral,' one of his sons remarked."

Recalling the crippling polio that struck him in 1921, Teddy's cousin, Franklin Roosevelt, once noted, "If you had spent two years in bed trying to wiggle your big toe, after that anything else would seem easy." The "anything else" in Roosevelt's case was, of course, the twelve years he served as president. Despite the Great Depression and Second World War, he projected a jovial self-assurance and utter fearlessness that radiated out to the people, inspiring them to follow his leadership.

What's compelling about FDR in retrospect is the almost total control he maintained over his public persona. As character-building as his paralysis proved to be, he worked overtime to conceal it. Reporters and photographers observed an unwritten rule to keep the disability secret, and appearances were planned with the president seated or able to reach a podium with minimal movement. Of more than 35,000 pictures taken of Roosevelt, just two show him in a wheelchair, while political cartoonists actually sketched him running or jumping.

As Hugh Gregory Gallagher explains in *FDR's Splendid Deception*, Roosevelt was both actor and politician. "He used his cigarette holder to suggest confidence and good cheer; his old-fashioned pince-nez glasses reminded people of their school-teachers and of Woodrow Wilson," Gallagher notes. "His old fedora campaign hat was as familiar as an old shoe; his naval cape expressed dignity and drama. The complete package of props, together with the characteristic tilt of the head, the wave of the hand, the laugh, the smile, made FDR seem to the American people as familiar, as close as a family member." The Fireside Chats, which Roosevelt delivered so effectively on radio to living rooms across the country, reinforced the human, almost intimate connection he tried to cultivate.

Deception about the president extended to the women other than Eleanor Roosevelt close to FDR. Although the couple remained legally wed, Eleanor's discovery of Franklin's affair with

Lucy Mercer during World War I resulted in a complicated marital relationship of separate bedrooms but similar political objectives for the two Roosevelts. While the First Lady devoted herself to her own work, travel, and causes, he combined activities as president with the off-duty conviviality he enjoyed with several women, including Margaret Suckley, Marguerite LeHand, Laura Delano, and the later-widowed Lucy Mercer Rutherford. From everything we now know, FDR was never very far from ladies other than the First Lady—four were with him in Warm Springs, Georgia, when he died in 1945—but the precise nature of each relationship remains the subject of rumor rather than fact.

FDR relaxed with feminine companions without fear of reporters communicating such news to the public. He called the shots about his personal coverage. At one press conference, with characteristic playfulness, he announced, "Where I am going I cannot tell you. When I am to get back I cannot tell you. And where I am going on my return I don't know. That's a lot of news, and it can't be released until I am ready." Setting the news agenda as he did kept the focus on the White House as the administration wanted, relegating reporters to the status of stenographers.

Running for president in 1932, the first of his four victorious campaigns, Roosevelt said, "The presidency is not merely an administrative office. That's the least of it. . . . It is preeminently a place of moral leadership." The political and journalistic climate that FDR did so much to influence continued the earlier trend of emphasizing the public performance and personality of the president while avoiding what might be considered the private life of the nation's highest official. What the phrase "moral leadership" means is less ambiguous in that environment because the lines between "public" and "private" are relatively clear.

For the past quarter-century, however, those lines have increasingly blurred. In today's political-media environment, anything seems to go, with the notion of privacy almost an anachronism. Particularly in the realms of health and sexual activity, two off-limit subjects for several decades, a president (or aspirant for the office) now endures scrutiny without defined limits. This stark change of approach—a shift from taboo to tell-all—is the consequence of several political and cultural causes that converged to create an entirely new ethos for the collection and circulation of personal information.

The traumas of the Vietnam War and Watergate raised suspicions about the veracity and virtue of two presidents, Lyndon Johnson and Richard Nixon. Those suspicions, which proved to be warranted, forced journalists covering government and politics to reconsider how they went about their work. Stenographic reporting seemed insufficient when confronted with statements that tested the truth and deeds that flouted the law.

The investigative efforts of Carl Bernstein and Bob Woodward of the *Washington Post* in revealing the tangled tale of Watergate influenced not only Nixon's resignation in 1974 but the way presidents—both future and past—would be treated and viewed. The impact of Bernstein and Woodward, especially their best-selling books *All the President's Men* (1974) and *The Final Days* (1976) about Nixon's final months in the White House, spread beyond journalism and altered the larger culture's receptivity to information previously deemed private. Once the barriers came down and the public seemed fascinated with what happened inside the corridors and other places of power, the unwritten rules about the legitimacy—or illegitimacy—of specific subjects dramatically changed.

In late 1975, a little over a year after Nixon left office, a Senate committee report revealed that "a close friend" of President John Kennedy was simultaneously "a close friend" of mob leader Sam Giancana. When reporters identified the "close friend" as a woman, Judith Campbell Exner, America's modern-day Camelot no longer seemed as enchanting as before. The image of the martyred president with the perfect family competed with stories of troubling recklessness and an insatiable appetite for extramarital liaisons. Not long after the Senate report appeared, newspaper and magazine reports linked Kennedy to several women other than his wife, forcing journalists to reconsider how they went about covering the private lives of high public officials. Was it fair to avoid tawdry reality at the same time a president tried to present an illusion of domestic bliss?

With Kennedy we also subsequently learned about his chancy

health and his long battle with Addison's disease and other ailments. The cheerful vigor he tried to project often masked excruciating pain and, at times, even problems with walking. As more details came out, reporters questioned their responsibility to scrutinize the physical condition of a president or someone seeking the office.

The more open environment for information that took shape in the mid-1970s has turned into the tell-all culture of today with its outpouring of highly personal memoirs and behind-the-scenes accounts about every aspect of life. In this respect, the White House is no different from Hollywood, Wall Street, or any other visible or powerful institution peopled by individuals the public wants to know more about.

As this probing behind images and façades rooted itself in communications, the process for electing presidents also changed, becoming more open to citizen involvement and less dependent on the decision making of party leaders. The new emphasis on primaries and caucuses put an end to smoke-filled rooms, where Democratic and Republican elders privately evaluated the strengths and weaknesses of White House hopefuls. The citizenry now learned about presidential candidates principally from the media. Among other things, these procedural reforms placed more responsibility on journalists to take the full measure of prospective presidents. Without three-dimensional profiles that included less flattering information, it became increasingly possible that the people would have a skewed perception of the nation's highest leader.

What happened in politics, government, and communications during the late 1960s and 1970s set in motion forces that transformed how Americans view their presidents. The consequences of the Vietnam War and Watergate cast a pall on the White House that shows no signs of disappearing. In addition, revisionist historical studies of the private and public transgressions of previous presidents abound and vie with contemporary accounts about an incumbent president's personal and professional comportment, whether virtuous or not.

Even before Ronald Reagan completed his eight years in the White House, nearly a dozen former members of his staff had

published memoirs questioning his work ethic, style of governance, and preference for comics rather than a newspaper's front
page. When one insider account revealed that an astrologer
friendly with Nancy Reagan helped plan the president's travel
schedule, people wondered aloud about not only the First Lady's
clout but her husband's reliance on outside advice and the quality of that counsel.

Reagan poked fun at himself for not letting the presidency
consume him, telling one reporter: "They say hard work never
killed anyone, but I figure, why take a chance?" Day-to-day details of administration were delegated to others. Speaking at
widely covered public events to stress a theme or issue was his
idea of what a president should do.

In *President Reagan: The Role of a Lifetime,* Lou Cannon, an
author and *Washington Post* correspondent who covered Reagan
as both governor of California and president, reports that White
House Chief of Staff James Baker delivered a briefing book to the
president the evening before an international economic summit
began in 1983. Since the meetings were taking place in the U.S.,
Reagan was responsible for presiding at the sessions and guiding
the discussions. The next morning, when Baker saw the briefing
book exactly where he left it, he asked the president why he
hadn't looked at it. "Well, Jim, *The Sound of Music* was on last
night."

For Ronald Reagan, being president was, indeed, playing a
role—a public performance that advanced his administration's
agenda. His "big picture" priorities often seemed to come from
the reassuring, good-defeats-evil scripts of the big screen. In his
acting days, he actually was cast as federal agent Brass Bancroft,
who in the 1940 film *Murder in the Air* protects "the Inertia Pro-
jector" from falling into enemy hands. Able to knock unfriendly
planes out of the air four miles away, the Hollywood-devised
technology bears a striking resemblance to the Strategic Defense
Initiative that he proposed as president in 1983.

SDI, of course, became popularly known as the "Star Wars"
program, enhancing the cinematic character of the project—and
the Reagan presidency. Interestingly, though, commitment to
SDI played a serious policy role in the demise of the Soviet

Union. Whether motivated by movie story-lines or political ideology or both, the personal origins of Reagan's commitment pale in comparison to the eventual outcome.

Although Reagan's two terms as president took place during the new period of openness following Watergate, his private life never aroused an inordinate amount of curiosity. There was some discussion of his distance from his children and his devout absence from church on Sunday. But the closeness of his relationship to his wife and his repeated invocation of America as a "city upon a hill," worthy of its own reverence, struck resonant chords with the public.

How he actually spent his time as president was another matter, and the subject of much concern. The memoirs of those around him and journalistic accounts based on interviews with insiders carried a common theme: Reagan's detachment from governing entrusted subordinates with more power than they deserved (witness the international shenanigans of Oliver North), and away from cameras or a stage he seemed very much alone. The smiling grandfatherly figure was, in reality, a distant relative we didn't really know.

Although sunny in outlook, square-shouldered in physique, and commanding in public, Ronald Reagan and Bill Clinton share little else in common, except the fact that each was twice-elected to the White House in consecutive decades. While a sense of mystery surrounded Reagan as president and person, it's almost as though we know too much about Clinton. Who cares about the leader of the free world's preference in underwear? Well, when a young woman on MTV inquired about this subject early in his first term, Clinton obliged with a response.

The world would learn much more about Clinton and his preferences during his scandal-marred second term. Like the Senate committee investigation in 1975 that launched the posthumous probing of John Kennedy's libidinous licentiousness, Independent Counsel Kenneth Starr's formal investigation of Clinton's past resulted in revelations about the president's relationship with Monica S. Lewinsky, sparking a media frenzy about it and related matters. This time, of course, the scrutiny involved a sitting president, and there were many more communications outlets pursuing the story with single-minded intensity.

Although charges of perjury, obstruction of justice, and abuse of power swirled around the White House, the tale of an incumbent president engaged in an extramarital affair with a woman half his age made some journalists and commentators pant after every scrap of information. Vigorous coverage, it was thought, might put to rest the lingering criticism that journalists looked the other way during Kennedy's time.

But determining precisely what deserves public scrutiny today presents serious ethical dilemmas. What can reporters do to achieve a sense of proportion between public and private concerns? How relevant is a president's financial condition? Are all health matters fair game? If a marriage continues despite a pattern of infidelity, is it anyone else's business other than the husband and wife's? How does the nation's leader interact with staff and go about the business of governing on a regular, away-from-cameras basis?

Such questions don't yield easy answers—and they shouldn't, especially at a time when there is more inclination to divulge personal information. When privacy had a more exact definition and mutually agreed boundaries, it was easier for a president to maintain control and the aura of power. Today the best a president and his staff can try to do is "spin" or manipulate their version of events in the most favorable way, with the results of such efforts enormously unpredictable.

Given the proliferation of journalistic sources during the past several years—all-news cable networks, Internet sites, specialized publications—the news cycle is no longer determined by a newspaper's final edition or the evening news program of a major television network. As the Clinton adminstration has demonstrated in this new technological environment, rapidly responding to a report at any time—what might be called "spincraft"—has now become as important as stagecraft. Though often dizzying for the citizenry, this spincraft assures a competing point of view that either contradicts or cushions potentially damaging information.

Ever since Bill Clinton emerged as a presidential candidate in

1992, he has been the focus of endless examination and controversy. Stories about affairs, avoiding the draft, and experimenting with marijuana served as a prelude to later reports about questionable business practices, a volcanic temper, and several other sexual encounters. Ironically, though, this public figure about whom we've learned so much remains in the view of his most respected biographer, David Maraniss, a human puzzle, always concealing aspects of his life so we won't see the whole person.

Writing in *The Clinton Enigma,* Maraniss observes, "All human beings have secrets, all have done things that they would prefer were not fully revealed to the world. The public life is built on half-truths, and it is natural for anyone, especially a politician, to try to present himself in the best light. . . . But with Clinton, the tension between reality and image, between what he is and what he wants to be, is so relentless that over the years it became habitual for him to withhold information—justifiably or not."

As the past several years teach, Clinton's moral compass points in several directions simultaneously. Language functions as both shield and sword, defensive and offensive weapons, as he tries to protect himself politically and personally. The impeachment imbroglio, however, brought into broad public view the secrecy and hypocrisy that observers of Clinton have known about since his years as governor of Arkansas.

The lingering, unanswerable question is: Why does Bill Clinton play this elaborate game of hide-and-seek, when he's aware the contemporary political and media climate has few, if any, reservations about revelations? Especially with an aggressive Independent Counsel investigation in process and before the settlement of the sexual harassment suit of Paula Jones against him, conducting the relationship with Monica Lewinsky is beyond reckless abandon. Despite the president's assertions that his privacy had been violated with disclosures of their misadventures, he had previously denied any unbecoming conduct and directed his staff and cabinet to support him. The so-called private matter had, in actuality, become public business when government workers began devoting their tax-paid time to vigorous defense of a lie.

Despite over a year of attention devoted to every aspect of this unseemly tale, Bill Clinton stands impeached by the House of Representatives, acquitted by the Senate—and roundly approved for his work as president in public opinion surveys. Why the continued backing amid such controversy? In part, he's the beneficiary of a robust economy and a post–Cold War world that is generally peaceful from an American perspective. (A Saddam Hussein in Iraq or a Slobodan Milosevic in Yugoslavia will always be dangerous to world order and deserve strategically targeted military force.) In addition, people recognize his intelligence, mastery of domestic policy, willingness to work, empathy, and heroic resilience. It's not so much a matter of condoning misbehavior and efforts to cover it up as discriminating among everything that's known about Clinton and basing a judgment on what matters the most. Character traits coexist with character flaws.

At a time that puts a premium on personality and performance to gain public attention, Clinton in a curious way has become the nation's Celebrity-in-Chief. Soap-opera scandals are nothing new to celebrities in other realms, with value judgments about private affairs of less concern than overall appeal. As long as Americans applaud the country's prosperity and basic direction, the president's combined efforts of staying the course and surviving in office offer a real-life drama with macabre fascination. All the late-night television jokes about the White House as the new set for a remake of the movie "Animal House" serve as comic relief—but also reinforce the notion of a president being a contemporary celebrity. Goose-pimple respect for the presidency can get lost in this relatively new atmosphere of less civic action, with its decline in voting, and more spectatorial passivity.

In this new climate, the atrophying allegiance to a party's principles and programs takes on particular significance. Emphasizing the individual political actor prompts more sustained scrutiny of the persona and how that persona might affect governance. With party discipline waning among citizens, it is only natural that concerns about what a public figure is "really like"—beyond the image and the spin—assumes added weight in judging electability and conduct in office.

Mark Twain once observed, "Every one is a moon, and has a dark side which he never shows to anybody." Prominence and power notwithstanding, presidents are really no different from anyone else. Now, however, they have to cope with the probable—yes, probable—disclosure of any fact or rumor that suggests "a dark side" or murky motive. Campaign consultants regularly ask White House hopefuls, "Are you ready to have everything you've ever done appear on the front page of the *Washington Post* and the *New York Times?*"

Moreover, as recent revelations about Jefferson and Kennedy make clear, even dead presidents don't rest in peace in the current climate. Shortly after genetic testing indicated that Jefferson likely fathered at least one child with a slave woman, stories appeared that Washington might have done likewise. To return to the time when Parson Weems mythologized Washington with invented stories about a cherry tree and never telling a lie serves neither history nor truth. But the opposite approach we see today emphasizes human failings in sensational, tabloidistic ways. A president's clay feet can trip us up in arriving at a balanced and comprehensive view of individual figures and the institution itself. Stressing the negative obscures the whole person and provokes cynicism about the office.

Harry Truman's view of the president as "two people"—the nation's leader and an imperfect person—showed uncommon common sense. In an interview for *Plain Speaking* after leaving the White House, he went on to explain: "When you get to be president, there are all those things, the honors, the twenty-one gun salutes, all those things, you have to remember it isn't for you. It's for the presidency, and you've got to keep yourself separate from that in your mind. If you can't keep the two separate, yourself and the presidency, you're in all kinds of trouble."

Truman is right from the perspective of a president. But keeping those two aspects separate is impossible for citizens because the human dimension remains a critical factor in what judgments we make about the residents of 1600 Pennsylvania Avenue. The White House by its nature combines the highest elected official's public work *and* private life in a single structure that functions as adminstrative office, ceremonial site, personal residence, and national symbol. Understanding any president demands a sense of proportion and measured scrutiny that acknowledges human complexity and mystery—and how they dance together.

Postscript

The scandal-scarred presidency of Bill Clinton provoked an outpouring of reflections on contemporary leadership and political life. This essay originally appeared in the spring 1999 issue of *Notre Dame Magazine,* not long after the impeachment and Senate trial of Clinton. The significance of previously private matters on public affairs had come to the forefront of everyone's attention with such force that an effort to provide a longer-range perspective on the human side of the presidency seemed in order.

Despite the extensive media coverage of Clinton's problems, public opinion surveys reflected strong, sustained approval of his performance as president throughout the months of the ordeal. With the federal budget in the black, welfare rolls down, income levels up, and crime, drug use, and teen pregnancy rates declining, it seemed as though Americans were willing to credit Clinton for the country's positive direction. Complicating any assessment of the president, however, were low judgments of his honesty, trustworthiness, and capacity for moral leadership. Clinton, who talked about "compartmentalization" between the public and the private, was the beneficiary of the appropriate circumstances to make such an argument.

The artist Salvador Dali once remarked, "In America Surrealism is invisible for all is larger than life." Interestingly, the word "surreal" kept appearing in reports and commentaries about the Clinton-Lewinsky affair and its aftermath. The unprecedented nature of the whole knotty (and nutty) experience left analysts of every stripe and pedigree groping in the dark for possible consequences on the presidency and its future in an anything-goes environment.

SEEKING EQUILIBRIUM AND
A CENTER THAT HOLDS

Given America's culture of freedoms and constancy of dynamism (often featuring change for the sake of change), going too far to excess—even to extremes—has become a recurring fact of our national life. For whatever reasons or causes, forces (usually economic, social, cultural, or political) collect energy and make moderating efforts an afterthought. By that time, to paraphrase Emerson, the forces are in the saddle, riding the people—with the consequences creating a new dynamic that often involves indecent liberties of one kind or another.

However, avoiding excess while seeking equilibrium has a venerable tradition of its own that bears remembering when we recognize the gathering strength of a phenomenon with a dubious or even dangerous future. From the Greek motto *meden agan*—nothing in excess—that was carved on the temple of Apollo at Delphi to the contemporary environmental concern of maintaining a deliberate as well as delicate balance of nature, one finds a continuum of thought and action that emphasizes the fertility of the middle ground and the desire for equipoise. Indeed, to stray too far afield from what is perceived to be common ground in litigious America can lead to a court case, with the judiciary serving—in the phrase of Woodrow Wilson—as "the balance wheel" in resolving the matter. Achieving justice requires equal weight on either side of the metaphorical scales.

Our constitutional system of governance—with its tripartite division of powers and, even more significantly, its process for checks and balances to circumscribe and limit each branch's power—owes at least a small conceptual debt to the Greek phi-losophers. Aristotle, in particular, gets some specific credit as an advocate of moderation and for seeking "the golden mean" be-tween extremes. In *The Nicomachean Ethics, Politics,* and else-where, Aristotle sets down in concrete terms a philosophy of pro-portion, which helped inspire the framers of the Constitution. In *Politics,* he refers back to *Ethics* to champion life in a mean: "For if what was said in the *Ethics* is true, that the happy life is the life according to virtue lived without impediment, and that virtue is a mean, then the life which is in a mean, and in a mean attain-able by every one, must be the best."

Especially in *Politics,* Aristotle argues that moderation leads to stability and harmony among people. The so-called "happy life" or "good life" can occur collectively, as long as individuals follow a middle course between whatever vices exist beyond the mean. The state, too, benefits when citizens moderately conduct them-selves:

> Those who think that all virtue is to be found in their own party principles push matters to extremes; they do not consider that disproportion destroys a state. A nose which varies from the ideal of straightness to a hook or snub may still be of good shape and agreeable to the eye; but if the excess be very great, all symmetry is lost, and the nose at last ceases to be a nose at all on account of some excess in one direction or defect in the other; and this is true of every other part of the human body. The same law of proportion equally holds in states. (Book V, Ch. 9)

Influential as Aristotle might have been on the authors of the Constitution and subsequent generations, Ancient Greece is light-years away from modern America, and his idealism about always striving to attain a mean seems, in its way, dreamily pla-tonic. Moreover, in the introduction to the Modern Library edi-tion of *Politics,* Max Lerner observes "that in history political equilibrium has been achieved only by the ebb and flow of revo-lutionary movements." In other words, as happened with the founding of the United States and numerous other countries since the eighteenth century, violent upheaval by revolution-minded extremists overturned an existing order that itself was perceived to be extremist in nature. The clash between opposing extremes created a new state or order, which then had to struggle for the stability that comes from equilibrium.

In subsequent years, abolitionists, suffragettes, advocates for civil rights across racial, ethnic, and gender lines, environmentalists (to name just a few challengers to the status quo) have internally contributed to the continuing "ebb and flow" of an America striving to be more faithful to the original principles of "Life, Liberty, and the pursuit of Happiness." By its nature, democracy (in Tocqueville's encompassing sense) promotes a climate for change, even though what Tocqueville saw as a "tyranny of the majority" can always inhibit efforts to achieve that change. However, for people in the movements noted above, the driving motivation of equalizing balance set them in motion in the first place. Difficulty, of course, arises at where precisely to draw the line—to avoid exacerbating a situation or pushing for change to an extreme that itself is destructively destabilizing.

Aristotle's blindness to the necessity of radical change in certain circumstances is—to apply his nomenclature—a "defect." However, his abiding principle of the need for proportionality is, in general, valuable for its measured—yes, deliberative—approach to personal and political conduct. Increasingly, consideration of a matter or conduct related to it in America takes place at either ends of the spectrum, leaving middle ground or area of commonality abandoned terrain. Synthesizing vital elements of the two opposing viewpoints into a coherent, acceptable, broadly beneficial mean is rejected as capitulation to the other side.

As noted previously, extreme multiculturalism competes today with equally militant European-tradition-is-the-only-American-tradition xenophobia, producing continuing conflicts that fail to acknowledge the value of working out an integrative approach combining the legitimate concerns of either side. Clearly there are dangers from overemphasis on specific racial or ethnic characteristics at the expense of some sense of national unity. Conversely, it is perilous and blindly limiting to fail to acknowledge the contributions of different cultures to a pluralistic nation with a long history of receiving—if not always welcoming—waves of immigrants. As Henry Louis Gates, Jr., remarks in *Loose Canons: Notes on the Culture Wars,* "Today, the mindless celebration of difference for its own sake is no more tenable than the nostalgic return to some monochrome homogeneity." Gates proposes "the search for a middle way." Mean-testing of the kind advocated in this chapter requires give-and-take and a studied effort at strategic consensus-building that balances diversity and unity. To stay encamped on either side with no movement in the other direction leaves any common ground barren— and without the possibility for growth that, ultimately, might enrich everyone concerned.

The Aristotelian emphasis on mean, proportion, and symmetry foreshadows (among other things) the stress on equilibrium fundamental to Newtonian physics and later to the economic thinking of Alfred Marshall in Victorian times. However, in neither case nor in more recent work across disparate fields does equilibrium suggest static simplicity without strong forces at play. With scarring phrasing, William Butler Yeats in his poem "The Second Coming" describes a civilization of extremes holding sway and the need for an anchoring center:

> Things fall apart; the center cannot hold;
> Mere anarchy is loosed upon the world. . . .

Yeats takes a recondite civilizational approach. More simply and germane to our subject, equilibrium thinking does not imply rumination on inactivity or (what would be even worse) mindless contentment with a never-changing status quo. Rather, it involves the critical survey of the spectrum of human thought and action, the recognition of the excesses that exist at either end of the spectrum, and seeking the mean that promises the most fruitful or purposeful direction for future thought and action. Rigidity can (and often does) stifle creativity, and absolutism— especially of whatever ideological or political knee-jerk variety—

is antithetical to America's democratic tradition of fostering pluralism and tolerance.

As earlier essays point out, an excessive or extreme action often provokes an excessive or extreme reaction that sparks continuing, unresolved tension or conflict. In correcting a problem or an injustice, remedial measures can go too far in the opposite direction, undercutting prospects for success that is both encompassing and enduring. Alas, the contemporary women's movement is an illustrative case study. What began in the 1960s as one of the many revolutions at that time to gain equal rights in education, the work-place, housing, and other realms took on a life of its own that, ultimately, resulted in a censorious and questioning backlash by many of those previously involved in the movement. In *"Feminism Is Not the Story of My Life,"* Elizabeth Fox-Genovese takes on what has become the dominant thinking and approach of feminism today, especially its elitism and distancing from the lives of women who try to balance work and home on a daily basis. As she notes:

> Frustrated by divisions within the feminist ranks, the more radical leaders have increasingly insisted that anyone who rejects their views is "anti-woman." And anyone who speaks of family values is necessarily defending the religious right. In *The Second Stage,* Betty Friedan made a valiant attempt to reintroduce the family at the heart of feminist programs, but, resoundingly, she failed to convert radical feminists. Ellen Willis, speaking for the radicals, announced that "the family is a dying beast" and denounced pro-family feminists as no feminists at all. (p. 30)

Later, Fox-Genovese mentions that such well-known feminists as Katie Roiphe and Naomi Wolf are "challenging feminist correctness from the inside. Roiphe and Wolf worry that feminist campaigns to impose 'correct' thought and behavior will curtail the freedoms, including sexual freedom, feminists have been fighting for." Taken to extremes, any viewpoint (conceived in an environment of freedom) can become dogmatic and threaten the spirit of freedom that originally animated the cause. Curiously, yet consistently, stasis occurs at the extremes rather than within the mean between those extremes.

In its way, Fox-Genovese's argument is similar to that of Arthur M. Schlesinger, Jr. (*The Disuniting of America*) or Robert Hughes (*Culture of Complaint*) in writing about multiculturalism or political correctness and Shelby Steele (*The Content of Our Character*) or Richard Rodriguez (*Hunger of Memory*) in discussing issues of race and ethnicity. These authors critically assess how far certain modes of thinking and action have been carried and their controversial consequences. However, responding to such work, the most extreme proponents of the positions in question have shrilly rejected this commentary as reactionary or worse, the rantings of the hopelessly unenlightened at a time when being right requires obeisance to the strict dogma of the far left. To be fair, a similar argument can easily be made coming from the other direction, with the dark tunnel vision of full-moon conservatives and the most devout followers of the Religious Right just as troubling as anything at the other pole. For someone trying to be dispassionate, human sympathy and compassion seem in short supply on either end of the spectrum. Doing good often takes a backseat to doing battle, however good might be defined.

Of course, one person's moderate stance is another's unacceptable alternative. Yet being inflexibly closed-minded can kill any cause, no matter the original motivation. In *The Twilight of Common Dreams: Why America Is Wracked by Culture Wars,* Todd Gitlin explains what has happened on the American left in recent years and why its current state seems so far removed from earlier objectives. A former president of Students for a Democratic Society who remains faithful to New Left tenets of the 1960s, Gitlin argues that some "Americans are obsessed with their racial, ethnic, religious, and sexual identities." This obsession with diversity leads to an overemphasis on particularity at the expense of an overarching, shared unity. Referring to many of the more prominent proponents of "identity politics" as "fundamentalists" (a label freighted with images of dangerous religious fanatics in distant lands) Gitlin, a professor of communications and culture at New York University, notes: "But what is a Left if it is not, plausibly at least, the voice of a whole people? For the Left as for the rest of America, the question is not whether to recognize the multiplicity of American groups, the variety of American communities, the disparity of American experiences. Those exist as long as people think they exist. The question is one of proportion. What is a Left without a commons, even a hypothetical one? If there is no people, but only peoples, there is no Left."

Yes. As with so many other subjects and concerns treated in this book, proportion is critical. To go too far either left or right leaves much—if not all—common ground vacant. Such an approach might seem ideologically and emotionally satisfying; however, it reduces the possibility of actually accomplishing very much. In recent American political history, Barry Goldwater's speech accepting the presidential nomination at the 1964 Republican Convention provides a lesson. In it the late Arizona senator uttered two sentences that today retain inflammatory power: "I would remind you that extremism in the defense of liberty is no vice. And let me remind you that moderation in the pursuit of justice is no virtue." In *The Making of the President, 1964,* Theodore H. White reported that Goldwater's own text had these sentences underlined for emphasis. White goes on to say the speech signaled to America and the world a "politics of no compromise."

Goldwater, of course, lost to Lyndon B. Johnson, and received only 38.5 percent of the popular vote. Goldwater's conservatism, however, ultimately gained the acceptance of a majority of voters with the election of Ronald Reagan as president in 1980 and Reagan's re-election in 1984. Although America had dramatically changed from 1964 to 1980 and faith in government had markedly declined in the aftershocks of the Vietnam War and Watergate, Reagan was different from Goldwater in how he positioned himself on the political spectrum and in the public mind. Sunny rather than severe, the former actor emphasized an all-American appeal, which brought millions of so-called

"Reagan Democrats" to his side. Despite core beliefs indistinguishable from Goldwater's, Reagan's engaging personality and essential pragmatism made him acceptable to a broad—albeit mostly white—constituency.

Even more overtly than Reagan and his encompassing city-on-a-hill Americanism, Bill Clinton discovered during the last two years of his first term (1995 and 1996) the political importance of being perceived as a centrist, able to combine ideas and practices of those regarded as being on the left or right. More significantly, he sought to avoid any identification with—in his often-used word—"extreme" thinking and action. Particularly after the April 1995 bombing of the Alfred P. Murrah Federal Building in Oklahoma City and with the media spotlight trained on government-hating fringe groups, Clinton repeatedly talked of "common ground" and the need for a "dynamic center" that would bring together citizens of varying perspectives.

To win the presidency in 1992 Clinton drew heavily on the argument advanced by E. J. Dionne, Jr., in his 1991 book *Why Americans Hate Politics*. Dionne saw the polarization over such matters as gender equality and the family or social compassion and personal self-reliance as creating a succession of "false choices" that never get resolved: "The false choices posed by liberalism and conservatism make it extremely difficult for the perfectly obvious preferences of the American people to express themselves in our politics. We are encouraging an 'either/or' politics based on ideological preconceptions rather than a 'both/and' politics based on ideas that broadly unite us." Most political questions involving the status and future of the American people at large do not lend themselves to a yes or no answer, let alone an either/or alternative, and Dionne cogently explained how liberals and conservatives dug themselves into positions that made reaching out to anyone with a different opinion acts of political contortionism few public figures were willing to try.

Like Gitlin in *The Twilight of Common Dreams*, Dionne sees the excesses of the left as influential in setting up barriers that block interchange with people of different viewpoints:

In short: The New Left, which had sought to deepen democracy, increasingly taught liberals antidemocratic lessons. The neoconservatives, who had wanted a more rational approach to social policy, increasingly taught them the futility of social policy.

In the end, it was the inability of liberals to articulate a coherent sense of the national interest that was decisive in creating a politics of false choices. When the poor are seen as a "special interest" while the wealthy are not, something very peculiar has happened to the national political dialogue. When such values as family and work are perceived as the exclusive province of one party to the political debate, the other party has clearly made some fundamental blunders. When the party of racial harmony creates conditions that encourage racial divisions, something is awry in its program. When constituencies who had gotten jobs, gone to college, bought houses, started businesses, secured health care, and retired in dignity because of government decided, of a sudden, that "government was the problem"—when this happened, it was clear a political revolution was in process. (p. 144)

Valuable as Dionne's thinking might have been in the 1992 campaign to delineate the ramifications of the ascent of conservatism, Clinton's focus on gays in the military as a first priority and, later, the unveiling of the 1,342-page "Health Security Act," which proposed to bring government much more directly into American health care, led the public to conclude that the president was really not all that different from the liberal, activist Democrats he had distanced himself from in getting elected. The mid-term elections of 1994, which resulted in Republican majorities in the Senate and House of Representatives, were as much a repudiation of Clinton as an endorsement of the philosophy and politics of the GOP.

However, self-preservation is a mind-concentrating pursuit, and beginning in 1995 Clinton made the political center his base of operation. By focusing on reducing the deficit, balancing the budget, overhauling welfare, fighting crime, controlling guns, and emphasizing family values (by endorsing the V-chip for television, school uniforms, and curfews for teenagers), this born-again centrist kept Congressional Republicans on his right and Congressional Democrats to his left in a continuing strategy to be perceived as the leader following a middle way with appeal crossing traditional ideological boundaries.

Although now in disrepute for dallying with a prostitute and declaiming incessantly to anyone who will listen his conceptual mastery of the political arts, the political consultant Dick Morris does deserve credit for plotting Clinton's course to its center point. Without invoking the name of Hegel or mentioning the dialectic process, Morris told Elizabeth Drew (for her book *Showdown: The Struggle between the Gingrich Congress and the Clinton White House*) that Clinton sought to be a synthesizer: "That means both activist government and the conservative view of government. Thesis is an active government, antithesis is the Republican, negative view of government. By synthesis he means the middle ground. . . . What the President is trying to do is to take one from Column A and one from Column B. It's been described as centrism, as triangulation, but it's not those. It's common ground. It's a synthesis of the common wisdom of this country. . . . "

Morris was interviewed in the summer of 1995. A year later and with the presidential election less than three months away, Clinton personally described his approach in his book *Between Hope and History: Meeting America's Challenges for the 21st Century*. Subordinating Morris's abstraction, the president focused directly on specific measures and their possible consequences:

> We say the era of big government is over, but we must not go back to an era of "every man for himself." We need government to do those things which are essential to giving us the tools we need to make the most of our own lives, to honoring our obligations to one another, to building a strong economy, to protecting the public health and our environment. We believe we can shrink the size of government, reduce its burden, and improve its ability to help Americans meet the challenges of the new era and protect our values. There is simply no evidence that Amer-

ica can be better off if we abandon our attempt to go forward together and leave America's future to the tender mercies of the global marketplace. (p. 90)

An exit survey following the 1996 election (in which Clinton won with 49 percent of the popular vote) found 47 percent of respondents saying they were "moderate," with 33 percent calling themselves "conservative" and 20 percent "liberal." A few weeks after his re-election (and with Morris banished to become, of all things, a pundit purveying some of the sharpest criticism of Clinton in print or on the airwaves) the president told the Democratic Leadership Council of the importance of creating "a new center" that avoids "the lukewarm midpoint between overheated liberalism and chilly conservatism." At the end of his first major speech since Election Day, Clinton said: "To make this democracy work, we must create a vital and dynamic center that is a place of action." (The phrase "vital center" was coined by historian Arthur M. Schlesinger, Jr., in 1948 and explained fully in his 1949 book *The Vital Center: The Politics of Freedom,* which sought to chart a workable middle course for liberal democracies between fascism on the right and communism to the left.)

The failure—if not tragedy—of Clinton's second term has been the preoccupation with scandals, both real and alleged, that have made it impossible to bring this "vital and dynamic center" to life in ways that might well have changed the American political landscape. At a time when powerful forces with strong ideological and institutional components push so many aspects of our politics to extremes, the presidency—with its unifying possibilities and the sense of command coming from the bully pulpit—could have served as a continuing and effective balancing mechanism. With the political parties having lost much of their clout for pluralistic coalition-building in the past few decades, special interests have marshaled their resources into campaigns and causes they think they can influence. These narrow, single-issue groups have had a definite impact on the candidates who get elected. As a Brookings Institution study found, senators and representatives identified as centrists declined from about one-third in each chamber in the 1970s to approximately one-tenth in the 1990s. Fewer members of Congress known for consensus-building means more polarization as well as the hiring of more ideologically minded staff members who are crucial in proposing legislation and devising strategy.

Moreover, the media play a significant role in driving politics from the center. News coverage, discussion programs, and ads typically revolve around conflict and controversy. Ever since Monica Lewinsky became a household name, coverage of the White House has been skewed in the direction of the president's personal affairs rather than affairs of state, where he could show off his "vital and dynamic center." As noted in an earlier chapter, arguments stressing consensus or agreement might shed more light, but the heat from incendiary claims and fiery exchanges hold an audience, and—alas—prove more entertaining. Despite the public's vocal displeasure of the amount of coverage devoted to allegations and facts about what the president finally referred to as his "relationship with Miss Lewinsky that was not appropriate," the citizenry kept reading and watching as the charges and countercharges circulated. Curiosity created a collective gapers' block diverting attention from matters of governance. As one columnist remarked: "Ironic, isn't it, that Clinton, the zealous apostle of the V-chip, has created a media environment where concerned parents don't dare let their children watch the nightly news?"

Despite prosperity, peace, and strong approval ratings, the fog of scandal prevented Clinton from staking out "the common ground" he repeatedly talked about to any lasting degree. Indeed, using the presidency as a bully pulpit for moral encouragement markedly declined because what has been reported about the messenger, with such feverish intensity, undercuts the meaning of most messages about pursuing the right course, the virtuous path. The legacy of a truly dynamic political center could—indeed, would—have been the most valuable "bridge to the twenty-first century" that Clinton built during his second term. Of course, it would not have been easy. Volatility of public opinion makes it difficult to pinpoint where people locate themselves at any given time, and—truth be known—each person's center is different, a place squarely in the eye of the beholder. Unfortunately, though, the opportunity vanished amid all of the investigations of personal and political wrongdoing that partisan adversaries and the news media kept uppermost in the public's mind.

When anti-smoking legislation was defeated in the Senate June 17, 1998, one commentator noted: "It was a total rejection of Clinton's theory of governing, his hope of finding common ground with realistic Republicans such as Arizona Sen. John McCain." Another post-mortem pointed out that "although Clinton is personally popular, his legal problems have weakened his legislative influence and ability to focus." A common-ground approach demands comity and goodwill, feelings in short supply in a frenzy of scandal and sniping.

Formidable as the challenge might be, a rational or civil centrism—what Colin Powell and others refer to as a "sensible center"—will help people deal with divisions and problems in a spirit of common cause that acknowledges the virtues of free-market capitalism *and* the social-justice obligations of government. Vigorously experimental and willing to pursue the involvement of those in the public and private sectors, such an approach promises something different from a mushy middle-of-the-roadism or a split-the-difference compromising. Above all, an effort of this kind—in politics and other realms as well—offers a chance of working where polar opposites meet and synthesizing the valuable features of each side into a cohesive whole. Bold moves can come from measured steps. Ideally, debates would take place about means—say, the most effective and efficient ways of accomplishing something—but *not* about goals, the results that solve or at least ameliorate problems. Difficult as it might be to achieve, this rational or civil centrism seeks the equilibrium or balance that comes from reasoned consensus. As a nation, it would help take us closer to the mean Aristotle and others have wisely, if theoretically, plotted.

At a time of instant gratification and declining participation in so many spheres of American life, any proposal that advocates conscientious, sustained effort to shape thought and action in a new, harmonious way might be considered wishful thinking, even a fool's errand. However, we do well to remember that equilibrium and equality share the common Latin word *aequus*, which means equal or the same. Seeking equilibrium in a climate of freedom is also, in its ways, the search for equality, a goal as old as the Republic itself.

Yet, despite all the pressures for the de-centering of America that surround us, there is reason for hope. In the 1998 study *One Nation, After All: What Middle-Class Americans Really Think About: God, Country, Family, Racism, Welfare, Immigration, Homosexuality, Work, the Right, the Left, and Each Other,* the sociologist Alan Wolfe writes:

> By moving beyond polls and surveys to more ethnographic attempts to uncover people's beliefs, I have found little support for the notion that middle-class Americans are engaged in bitter cultural conflict with each other over the proper way to live. Middle-class people are not, in their cosmopolitan liberalism, out of touch with America and its core values. But nor are they so conservative that they have turned their backs on the problems of the poor and excluded. Neither determined secularists nor Christian-firsters, middle-class Americans have come to accept religious diversity as a fact of American life. Reluctant to pass judgment, they are tolerant to a fault, not about everything—they have not come to accept homosexuality as normal and they intensely dislike bilingualism—but about a surprising number of things, including rapid transformations in the family, legal immigration, multicultural education, and the separation of church and state. Above all moderate in their outlook on the world, they believe in the importance of leading a virtuous life but are reluctant to impose values they understand as virtuous for themselves on others; strong believers in morality, they do not want to be considered moralists. (p. 278)

As a new century and millennium dawn, America stands alone among other countries for its economic and military power and for its global cultural influence, principally through the various forms of media and their popular culture appeal. Satisfying as that status might be to someone's national pride, there still exists what Louis Brandeis identified almost a century ago as "the curse of bigness," the going too far in one or another direction because our freedom, democracy, and prosperity make that course—and curse—possible. America's future health and standing demand that each of us become something of an equilibrist, as we collectively do a balancing act and search for a center—of creativity and civility—that holds and endures.

ACKNOWLEDGMENTS

James Langford, the Director of the University of Notre Dame Press, is a patient yet persistent person. We first talked about a volume on the theme of going to excess in America in the early 1990s. Since then, four book projects of one kind or another have delayed completion of this one. Jim, however, remained characteristically encouraging as individual essays appeared, and I am words-fail-me grateful for his counsel and support. This is the fifth book I have happily done for the Notre Dame Press, and Jim is the principal reason for this long association. In addition, Jeff Gainey, Associate Director of the Press, never lost hope about playing a critical role in publishing this book, and I appreciate all of his efforts and enthusiasm. Once again, Carole Roos made stylistic changes and offered substantive suggestions for which I'm very thankful.

Michael Schaffer, the book editor of the *Philadelphia Inquirer* (whose doctorate in American history from Yale gives him exemplary background with which to deal with publishing today) generously offered his advice about this book's subject as the first chapter came into being. In recent years, Mike and Elizabeth Taylor, the admirably literate literary editor of the *Chicago Tribune*, let me read and review several books pertinent to this one. I am grateful to them and to four other editors at newspapers—Mike Leary at the *Philadelphia Inquirer*, Chris Chinlund at the *Boston Globe*, and Marcia Lythcott and John Twohey at the *Chicago Tribune*. Some sentences or paragraphs from pieces written for them seemed worth repeating here in either the essays or postscripts.

Walt Collins, editor emeritus of *Notre Dame Magazine,* and Kerry Temple, the current editor of the magazine, allowed me to work on articles important to this book. Their editorial skills helped sharpen these essays, making them more direct and complete.

Thomas J. Stritch, Professor Emeritus of American Studies, read the first-draft version of many of the chapters, noting problem areas or lines to pursue. Dedicating this book to Tom is a small expression of gratitude for nearly twenty years of wise counsel and editorial advice.

Max Lerner died on June 5, 1992; however, his thinking pervades several of these essays. I grew up reading Lerner's syndicated columns and books, romantically as well as stubbornly hoping that someday somewhere I might be able to combine journalism and academic work as he so effectively did. When by fate or good fortune Lerner came to Notre Dame in 1982 for a two-year stint as the W. Harold and Martha Welch Visiting Professor of American Studies, we ended up working together closely, even jointly teaching a class one semester. Max's restless mind and rare ability to draw connections among seemingly disparate aspects of—in the title of his widely praised study—*America as a Civilization* helped pushed me into new areas of inquiry. To serve with Stephen Lerner as Max's literary executor is one way of trying to show my thanks to a wonderful and influential man. The dedication of this book is another.

Mark Roche, Dean of the College of Arts and Letters at Notre Dame, immediately took an interest in this project and kindly helped make its completion possible. Notre Dame's Institute for Scholarship in the Liberal Arts provided support for the presentation of "America and Multiculturalism" at an academic conference in Italy.

With characteristic thoughtfulness and generosity, Reverend Theodore M. Hesburgh, C.S.C., President Emeritus of Notre Dame, provided reports and publications that proved valuable in composing several essays. Richard W. Conklin, Associate Vice President of University Relations at Notre Dame, also passed along publications of more than putative interest.

Nancy Kegler, the administrative assistant in the Department of American Studies and the Program in Journalism, Ethics, and Democracy, skillfully—and cheerfully—turned hundreds of pencil-scribbled pages into neatly processed typescript. Being chairman of the department since 1991 and director of the program since 1997 while trying to keep up with teaching and writing assignments has been possible in large measure because of her diligence and efficiency. She deserves more than a few words of thanks, as does Courtenay Myers, a model research assistant.

Judith Roberts Schmuhl and Michael Robert Schmuhl put up with the composition of another book in our home that also serves as a writer's refuge. Their admonitions about the teetering towers of books and messy mélange of magazines and newspapers cluttering several rooms have been heard and heeded. I promise to reform—right after I am finished with the next book.

WORKS CITED

Introduction

Heller, Joseph. *Catch-22.* New York: Simon and Schuster, 1961.
Potter, David M. *People of Plenty: Economic Abundance and the American Character.* Chicago: University of Chicago Press, 1954.
Thoreau, Henry David. *Walden and Civil Disobedience,* ed. Owen Thomas. New York: Norton, 1966.
Veblen, Thorstein. *The Theory of the Leisure Class.* In *The Portable Veblen,* ed. Max Lerner. New York: Viking, 1948.

Life, Liberty, and the Pursuit of Excess

Bok, Sissela. *Mayhem: Violence as Public Entertainment.* Reading, Mass.: Addison-Wesley, 1998.
Corwin, Norman. *Trivializing America: The Triumph of Mediocrity.* Secaucus, N.J.: Lyle Stuart, 1983.
Franklin, Benjamin. *The Autobiography of Benjamin Franklin and Selections from His Other Writings.* New York: Modern Library, 1944.
Gard, Wayne. *The Great Buffalo Hunt.* New York: Knopf, 1959.
Ginger, Ray. *Age of Excess: The United States from 1877–1914.* 2nd ed. Prospect Heights, Ill.: Waveland Press, 1975.
Hagedorn, Hermann. *Roosevelt in the Bad Lands.* Boston: Houghton Mifflin, 1921.
Jefferson, Thomas. *Thomas Jefferson on Democracy,* ed. Saul K. Padover. New York: New American Library, 1939.
Johnson, Paul. *A History of the American People.* New York: Harper-Collins, 1998.
Lerner, Max. *The Age of Overkill.* New York: Simon and Schuster, 1962.
Limerick, Patricia Nelson. *The Legacy of Conquest: The Unbroken Past of the American West.* New York: Norton, 1987.
Marks, Paula Mitchell. *In a Barren Land: American Indian Dispossession and Survival.* New York: William Morrow, 1998.

Peacock, Doug. *Bison: Distant Thunder.* New York: Takarajima Books, 1995.

Powers, Ron. *The Beast, the Eunuch, and the Glass-Eyed Child.* San Diego: Harcourt Brace Jovanovich, 1990.

Riis, Jacob A. *How the Other Half Lives: Studies among the Tenements of New York.* New York: Dover, 1971.

Sargent, Lyman Tower, ed. *Extremism in America: A Reader.* New York: New York University Press, 1995.

Sinclair, Andrew. *Era of Excess: A Social History of the Prohibition Movement.* New York: Harper and Row, 1964.

Smith, Henry Nash. *Virgin Land: The American West as Symbol and Myth.* 2nd ed. Cambridge, Mass.: Harvard University Press, 1978.

Stannard, David E. *American Holocaust: The Conquest of the New World.* New York: Oxford University Press, 1992.

Steinbeck, John. *America and Americans.* New York: Viking Press, 1966.

Tannen, Deborah. *The Argument Culture: Moving from Debate to Dialogue.* New York: Random House, 1998.

Trachtenberg, Alan. *The Incorporation of America: Culture and Society in the Gilded Age.* New York: Hill and Wang, 1982.

Turner, Frederick Jackson. *The Frontier in American History.* New York: Holt, 1947.

Twain, Mark, and Charles Dudley Warner. *The Gilded Age: A Tale of Today.* New York: New American Library, 1969.

White, Richard. *"It's Your Misfortune and None of My Own": A New History of the American West.* Norman: University of Oklahoma Press, 1991.

White, Theodore H. *America in Search of Itself: The Making of the President, 1956–1980.* New York: Harper and Row, 1982.

The Unsettling of America

Baker, Nicholson. *Vox.* New York: Random House, 1992.

Ellis, Bret Easton. *American Psycho.* New York: Vintage Books, 1991.

Lopez, Barry. *Crow and Weasel.* San Francisco: North Point Press, 1990.

Twain, Mark. *Adventures of Huckleberry Finn.* New York: Norton, 1962.

———. *The Adventures of Tom Sawyer.* New York: Washington Square Press, 1950.

America and Multiculturalism

Aristotle. *Politics.* New York: Modern Library, 1943.

Atlas, James. *Battle of the Books: The Curriculum Debate in America.* New York: Norton, 1992.

Codrescu, Andrei. *Road Scholar: Coast to Coast Late in the Century.* New York: Hyperion, 1993.

Crèvecoeur, J. Hector St. John de. *Letters from an American Farmer.* New York: E. P. Dutton, 1957.

DuBois, W. E. B. *The Souls of Black Folk.* Chicago: McClurg, 1903.

Fitzgerald, F. Scott. *The Crack-Up,* ed. Edmund Wilson. New York: New Directions, 1945.

Gates, Henry Louis. *Loose Canons: Notes on the Culture Wars.* New York: Oxford University Press, 1992.

Geyer, Georgie Anne. *Americans No More.* New York: Atlantic Monthly Press, 1996.

Graff, Gerald. *Beyond the Culture Wars: How Teaching the Conflicts Can Revitalize American Education.* New York: Norton, 1992.

Hughes, Robert. *Culture of Complaint: The Fraying of America.* New York: Oxford University Press, 1993.

Hunter, James Davison. *Culture Wars: The Struggle to Define America.* New York: Basic Books, 1991.

Kerouac, Jack. *On The Road.* New York: Penguin, 1976.

Lerner, Max. *America as a Civilization.* New York: Simon and Schuster, 1957.

Melville, Herman. *Redburn: His First Voyage.* Evanston and Chicago: Northwestern University Press and the Newberry Library, 1969.

Moon, William Least Heat. *Blue Highways.* Boston: Little, Brown, 1982.

Phillips, Kevin. *Boiling Point: Democrats, Republicans, and the Decline of Middle-Class Prosperity.* New York: Random House, 1993.

———. *The Politics of Rich and Poor: Wealth and the American Electorate in the Reagan Aftermath.* New York: Random House, 1990.

Schlesinger, Arthur M., Jr. *The Disuniting of America: Reflections on a Multicultural Society.* New York: Norton, 1992.

Takaki, Ronald. *From Different Shores.* New York: Oxford University Press, 1987.

Taylor, Charles. *Multiculturalism and "The Politics of Recognition."* Princeton: Princeton University Press, 1992.

Tocqueville, Alexis de. *Democracy in America,* ed. J. P. Mayer. New York: Harper and Row, 1966.

Twain, Mark. *Adventures of Huckleberry Finn.* New York: Norton, 1962.

Walzer, Michael. "What Does It Mean to Be an 'American'?" In *The American Intellectual Tradition,* ed. David A. Hollinger and Charles Capper. 2nd ed. New York: Oxford University Press, 1993.

Whitman, Walt. *The Complete Poetry and Selected Prose,* ed. James E. Miller, Jr. Boston: Houghton Mifflin, 1959.

Zangwill, Israel. *The Melting Pot, Drama in Four Acts.* New York: Macmillan, 1909.

Allies or Enemies?
The Uneasy Relationship between Blacks and Jews

Berman, Paul, ed. *Blacks and Jews: Alliances and Arguments.* New York: Delacorte Press, 1994.

Branch, Taylor. *Parting the Waters: America in the King Years, 1954–63.* New York: Simon and Schuster, 1988.

———. *Pillar of Fire: America in the King Years, 1963–65.* New York: Simon and Schuster, 1998.

Drake, St. Clair, and Horace R. Cayton. *Black Metropolis: A Study of Negro Life in a Northern City.* New York: Harcourt, Brace, 1945.

DuBois, W. E. B. *The Souls of Black Folk.* Chicago: McClurg, 1903.

Kaufman, Jonathan. *Broken Alliance: The Turbulent Times between Blacks and Jews in America.* New York: Scribner, 1988.

Lippmann, Walter. *Public Opinion.* New York: Harcourt, Brace, 1922.

Reed, Ishmael. *Airing Dirty Laundry.* Reading, Mass.: Addison-Wesley, 1993.

Terkel, Studs. *Race: How Blacks and Whites Think and Feel about the American Obsession.* New York: New Press, 1992.

Wright, Richard. *Black Boy.* New York: Harper and Row, 1966.

Running Scared

Kennedy, Paul. *The Rise and Fall of the Great Powers: Economic Change and Military Conflict from 1500 to 2000.* New York: Random House, 1987.

Mills, Nicolaus. *The Triumph of Meanness: America's War against Its Better Self.* Boston: Houghton Mifflin, 1997.

Coping with Hyperdemocracy and Hypercommunications

Fallows, James. *Breaking the News: How the Media Undermine American Democracy.* New York: Pantheon Books, 1996.

Gates, Bill. *The Road Ahead.* New York: Viking, 1995.

Grossman, Lawrence. *The Electronic Republic: Reshaping Democracy in the Information Age.* New York: Viking, 1995.

Halberstam, David. *The Powers That Be.* New York: Knopf, 1979.

Mathews, David. *Politics for People: Finding a Responsible Public Voice.* Urbana: University of Illinois Press, 1994.

Phillips, Kevin. *Arrogant Capital: Washington, Wall Street, and the Frustration of American Politics.* Boston: Little, Brown, 1994.

Salvador, Michael, and Patricia M. Sias, eds. *The Public Voice in a Democracy at Risk.* Westport, Conn.: Praeger, 1998.

Schmuhl, Robert. *Demanding Democracy.* Notre Dame, Ind.: University of Notre Dame Press, 1994.

White, Theodore H. *America in Search of Itself: The Making of the President 1956–1980.* New York: Harper and Row, 1982.

Being President When Anything Goes

Bernstein, Carl, and Bob Woodward. *All the President's Men.* New York: Simon and Schuster, 1974.

Britton, Nan. *The President's Daughter.* New York: Elizabeth Ann Guild, 1927.

Cannon, Lou. *President Reagan: The Role of a Lifetime.* New York: Simon and Schuster, 1991.

Gallagher, Hugh Gregory. *FDR's Splendid Deception.* New York: Dodd, Mead, 1985.

Maraniss, David. *The Clinton Enigma: A Four-and-a-Half-Minute Speech Reveals the President's Entire Life.* New York: Simon and Schuster, 1998.

Miller, Merle. *Plain Speaking: An Oral Biography of Harry Truman.* New York: Berkley Publishing, 1973.

Shogan, Robert. *The Double-Edged Sword: How Character Makes and Ruins Presidents, from Washington to Clinton.* Boulder, Colo.: Westview Press, 1999.

Smith, Gene. *When the Cheering Stopped: The Last Years of Woodrow Wilson.* New York: Morrow, 1964.

Woodward, Bob, and Carl Bernstein. *The Final Days.* New York: Simon and Schuster, 1976.

Seeking Equilibrium and a Center That Holds

Aristotle. *The Nicomachean Ethics.* Oxford: Oxford University Press, 1980.

——. *Politics.* New York: Modern Library, 1943.

Clinton, Bill. *Between Hope and History: Meeting America's Challenges for the 21st Century.* New York: Times Books, 1996.

Dionne, E. J., Jr. *Why Americans Hate Politics.* New York: Simon and Schuster, 1991.

Drew, Elizabeth. *Showdown: The Struggle between the Gingrich Congress and the Clinton White House.* New York: Simon and Schuster, 1996.

Fox-Genovese, Elizabeth. *"Feminism Is Not the Story of My Life": How Today's Feminist Elite Has Lost Touch with the Real Concerns of Women.* New York: Anchor Books, 1997.

Gates, Henry Louis, Jr. *Loose Canons: Notes on the Culture Wars.* New York: Oxford University Press, 1992.

Gitlin, Todd. *The Twilight of Common Dreams: Why America Is Wracked by Culture Wars.* New York: Metropolitan Books, 1995.

Hughes, Robert. *Culture of Complaint: The Fraying of America.* New York: Oxford University Press, 1993.

Rodriguez, Richard. *Hunger of Memory: The Education of Richard Rodriguez.* Boston: D. R. Godine, 1982.

Schlesinger, Arthur M., Jr. *The Vital Center: The Politics of Freedom.* Boston: Houghton Mifflin, 1949.

——. *The Disuniting of America: Reflections on a Multicultural Society.* New York: Norton, 1992.

Steele, Shelby. *The Content of Our Character: A New Vision of Race in America.* New York: St. Martin's Press, 1990.

White, Theodore H. *The Making of the President, 1964.* New York: Atheneum, 1965.

Wolfe, Alan. *One Nation, After All: What Middle-Class Americans Really Think About: God, Country, Family, Racism, Welfare, Immigration, Homosexuality, Work, the Right, the Left, and Each Other.* New York: Viking, 1998.